D1152746

proclamation 2

**Aids for Interpreting the
Lessons of the Church Year**

lesser
festivals 1

Saints' Days and
Special Occasions

Richard L. Thulin

editors: Elizabeth Achtemeier · Gerhard Krodel · Charles P. Price

FORTRESS PRESS   PHILADELPHIA

Library of Congress Cataloging in Publication Data (Revised)

Main entry under title:

Proclamation 2.

Consists of 24 volumes in 3 series designated A, B, and C which correspond to the cycles of the three year lectionary plus 4 volumes covering the lesser festivals. Each series contains 8 basic volumes with the following titles: Advent-Christmas, Epiphany, Lent, Holy Week, Easter, Pentecost 1, Pentecost 2, and Pentecost 3.
    CONTENTS: [etc.]—Series C: [1] Fuller, R. H. Advent-Christmas. [2] Pervo, R. I. and Carl III, W. J. Epiphany—Thulin, R. L. et al. The lesser festivals. 4 v.
    1. Bible—Homiletical use. 2. Bible—Liturgical lessons, English.
[BS534.5.P76]   251   79–7377
ISBN 0–8006–4079–9 (ser. C, v. 1)

8277D80   Printed in the United States of America   1–1393

Contents

Editor's Foreword   5

St. Andrew, Apostle (November 30)   7

St. Thomas, Apostle (December 21)   14

St. Stephen, Deacon and Martyr (December 26)   21

St. John, Apostle and Evangelist (December 27)   28

The Holy Innocents, Martyrs (December 28)   35

The Name of Jesus (January 1)   42

The Confession of St. Peter (January 18)   49

The Conversion of St. Paul (January 25)   57

Editor's Foreword

One of the benefits of the liturgical movement is the realization that in addition to the OT "cloud of witnesses" who did not receive what was promised (Heb. 11:39—12:1), there is also surrounding us a NT cloud of witnesses whose testimony and faith should be celebrated today. But there is a problem. The very word "witness" comes from the language of lawcourts and implies absolute truthfulness. The truth is, for instance, that through its appointed Gospel, the liturgical festival of St. John, Apostle and Evangelist, presupposes that the Beloved Disciple is identical with John the son of Zebedee and with the author of the Fourth Gospel. Yet modern scholarship would vigorously dispute such identity. So then, what and whom are we celebrating—a nameless disciple whom Jesus loved, an anonymous author, or one of the Twelve who was identical with neither? Or again, the assigned Gospel for the festival of the Confession of St. Peter, a festival which heretofore had not been celebrated in my particular tradition, ends with Matt. 16:19. Thus the congregation hears, "you are Peter," but does not hear what for Matthew is equally important: "you are a stumbling block" (16:23). In the First Gospel, Simon Bar Jona is both rock and stumbling block, but the Lutheran liturgical committee cut off the lesson at v. 19. In short, warning flags need to be raised against uncritical acceptance of liturgical traditions, and are raised repeatedly within the following pages. Preaching on the Lesser Festivals demands that the historical witness and the theological witness be clearly distinguished by the preacher.

In the following pages Richard Thulin, Ulrich Professor of the Art of Preaching at Gettysburg Seminary, interprets the lessons as assigned in the Lutheran lectionary. He does so in a scholarly manner and with homiletical concern. The Lesser Festivals provide the grid by which the sermon aids are here developed. As much as possible the homiletical themes are developed, properly, in relation to the texts.

5

The Lesser Festivals should be occasions for providing us with encouragement and examples. They should be reminders of the unity and continuity of the church, and a witness to and a joyful acknowledgment of the grace of God in Jesus Christ.

Gettysburg, Pa.   GERHARD KRODEL

St. Andrew, Apostle

NOVEMBER 30

Lutheran	Roman Catholic	Episcopal
Ezek. 3:16–21		Deut. 30:11–14
Rom. 10:10–18	Rom. 10:9–18	Rom. 10:8b–18
John 1:35–42	Matt. 4:18–22	Matt. 4:18–22

November 30 is celebrated as the day on which Andrew, according to tradition, was martyred in Achaia. He is supposed to have been crucified by the Romans on an X-shaped cross (decussate, the number ten) with arms bound rather than nailed. It is believed that his death came after extensive missionary activity among Gentiles in the lands bordering the Aegean and Black Seas. This feast seems to have been observed in the East as early as the fourth century. It was adopted by Rome in the sixth century. Andrew is the patron saint of Scotland and Russia and is held in special honor in Greece.

EXEGESIS

First Lesson: Ezek. 3:16–21. An immediate problem facing the exegete of this passage is the verbal identity between vv. 16–19 here and vv. 7–9 in chap. 33. Both sections refer to the same event, but there are differences of judgment as to which section is the original one. A decision seems important because we would like to know whether Ezekiel was first called as a prophet and then later as a "watchman," or whether he was called both as a prophet and a watchman at the same time (the tasks are different). Most likely vv. 16–21 of chap. 3 constitute a version of Ezekiel's second call which has been attached to the report of his first call (33:7–9 is the original section). According to this decision, the prophet's work took on the new dimension of "watchman" later in his career (when the hopes of the exiles among whom he preached had almost fully collapsed). In

7

either case, the text for St. Andrew, Apostle, presents Ezekiel as one called to the office of "watchman for Israel" as an extension of his call to be a prophet.

The task of the watchman is a familiar one in OT writings. Passages such as 2 Sam. 18:24–27 and 2 Kings 9:17–20 graphically describe the watchman's activities and indicate the necessity both of his presence and of the accuracy and promptness of his report. Also familiar in the OT are references to the prophets as watchmen (Hab. 2:1; Hos. 9:8; Jer. 6:17). The prophet as watchman is essential for the security of the people, and he must be both alert and faithful to his assignment.

As a watchman Ezekiel is obligated to report ("give warning"), and he must be persistent in carrying out his duty. Indeed, he will be held personally responsible for any negligence. But Ezekiel's appointment (he was neither elected nor a volunteer) contained a new characteristic. Ezekiel was to proclaim a personal word, a warning to individual men and women. His report was not to be simply a shout into the air or a general address given once to whoever happened to be in the area. His warning was to be a particular word for a particular person (notice the consistent references to "his"). Ezekiel is to seek out his people and is to address them in keeping with their situation (their needs).

It is interesting to note that Ezekiel's duty is completed with the communication of the particular word. Whether or not the "wicked man" or the "righteous man turned from his righteousness" pays attention to Ezekiel to the extent that he is reoriented is not Ezekiel's responsibility.

"Wickedness" or "turning from righteousness" seems to involve far more than disdain for the law. It has more to do with affirming or denying the then-and-there activity of God to establish a new covenant nation. "Wickedness" is only the symptom of a much deeper rejection, a denial of God's present work to reconstitute his people.

It should also be noted that the warning Ezekiel is to give on behalf of God is a complicated one. It is God who commands the prophet to warn the people. But God is also the One about whom the people are to be warned. God both threatens and warns. Enemies don't do this. God's purpose is to save.

Second Lesson: Rom. 10:10–18. It seems clear that this text was selected for St. Andrew, Apostle, because of what it says about the apostolate (particularly in vv. 14–17). An apostle is one who is sent forth (from *apo-stellein,* "to send forth") and thus authorized to preach Christ as a central function, and to preach Christ primarily to people who have not yet heard of him. The text stresses the importance of this "apostolic" ("sent forth") work of preaching Christ. Justification and salvation depend upon faith, faith depends upon preaching, and preaching depends upon the God who sends.

Several possibilities have been put forth as to Paul's purpose in the four-point argument of vv. 14–15. Two of them fit well into the general description of the apostolate. One suggestion is that Paul is arguing for a gentile mission. The emphasis here is on the people who "have never heard" (v. 14). A second suggestion is that Paul is strengthening the case for an apostolic or authorized ministry. Here the emphasis is on the ones "who are sent" (v. 15). Both of these suggestions may be productive in providing a context for the apostolate theme, but neither of them is wholly satisfactory. The argument in vv. 14 and 15 is part of a larger argument, one which has to do with Israel's rejection of Christianity. Paul's central claim is that Israel has no excuse. Faith comes from hearing, hearing comes from preaching, and preachers have definitely been sent. If there is a fault, it is the fault of unbelief. While this theme of failure does not necessarily promote a positive emphasis on Christian mission, its content does emphasize the universality of God's plan. Preaching Christ is intended for nothing less than the whole world. This universality is highlighted in the text by Paul's reference to "the same Lord" who is "Lord of all." It is further emphasized by his reference in v. 18 to Ps. 19:4. The "voice" quoted in v. 18 is the voice of the heavens and of the firmament. The preaching of the gospel, Paul says, is as universal as are the works of nature which tell the "glory of God" (Ps. 19:1).

V. 10 sets up the relation between faith (implied by justification) and salvation and provides the base for Paul's ensuing argument. But v. 10, in tandem with vv. 8 and 9, is of interest in itself. V. 9 alludes to a creedal formula, that is, "Jesus is Lord" for "God raised him from the dead." The two references in vv. 9–10 to "confession with lips" (and to the "word . . . on your lips" in v. 8) surely refer to the profession of faith made at baptism (and to the content of instruction which preceded it). Vv. 9 and 10 also connect faith and confession ("believing" and "confessing"). Faith and confession are simultaneous deeds. "Faith" is always "faith in." It has a dogmatic character inasmuch as it is acceptance of a word (the "word of faith" in v. 8). It is not piety, nor trust in God in general.

Gospel: John 1:35–42. This text contains three strands that are appropriate to a celebration of St. Andrew, Apostle. The first of these is the one which describes his call to discipleship and his first missionary activity as an apostle. Andrew is shown to be obedient both to John the Baptist and to Jesus. He is also shown acting out the apostolic life by finding his brother Simon Peter and bringing him to Jesus by way of the proclamation that Jesus is the Messiah.

The account is filled with significant words and phrases. The word "follow" signifies better than any other the dedication of discipleship (cf. 12:26; 21:19–22). The word "come" describes faith (5:40; 6:37, 45). "Stay" means both to tarry as a guest and to remain as a disciple. Within a few hours Jesus is called both Rabbi and Messiah (as on the next day, vv. 43–50, he is called both King of Israel and Son of God). The rapid occurrence of such charged language indicates that there is more going on here than the simple retelling of a historical event (this is also indicated by the differences between John's Gospel and the synoptics in regard to the calling of the disciples). It is as though in a single brief scene we are shown a glimpse of the whole life of discipleship, of both its qualities and its profession extended over a long period of time. More specifically, what we see perhaps is the entire span of Andrew's ministry, the center of its activity and confession, as well as its beginning.

There are several points of unclarity in these few verses. The second disciple referred to in the text is not identified. Many suggest that it is John, others Philip. The "tenth hour" in v. 39 could simply mean 4:00 P.M., or it could mean symbolically the "hour of fulfillment." The word "first" in v. 41 is also ambiguous. Most likely it means that as his first activity of the following day Andrew sought Peter.

A second strand in this text appropriate to the celebration of St.

Andrew, Apostle, is the mystery of the One whom Andrew "followed." It is expressed in the titles Lamb of God (the beloved Son, the servant of Yahweh, the victim without blemish) and Messiah (the expected one, the anointed one, the Christ). It is also expressed in Jesus' words to Simon Peter. The text seems to imply that Jesus knew Simon's name without asking. Moreover, the evangelist has Jesus renaming Simon before they have even spoken. (In Matthew's account this event does not occur until much later in Jesus' ministry and only then following Peter's confession—Matt. 16:16–18). The Jesus that Andrew follows is clearly remarkable—and yet he appears as a Jewish rabbi.

The third strand in this text appropriate to the celebration of St. Andrew, Apostle, is the work of John the Baptist, the one through whom Andrew comes to Jesus. The account holds up two important facts about John. One is the fact that people did come to believe in Jesus through him (the Baptist's purpose according to 1:7). The other is the fact that he indeed "bore witness that this is the Son of God" (1:34). He bore witness both by his words and by surrendering his own disciples to Jesus.

HOMILETICAL INTERPRETATION

Liturgically, the central theme for this celebration is proclamation. The appointed texts give life to that theme. Mission is both a pastoral and a congregational function, but in most cases it is the mission of the congregation that will provide the focus for the sermon. All Christians are involved in mission because they "follow" Jesus (the Greek word *akolouthein* is an active term; it is not a concept). More specifically, confession is always connected to faith. This connection is dramatically enacted at baptism. The Christian is always one who "believes in his heart" *and* "confesses with his lips."

Proclamation is an activity of people who are sent. (Ezekiel is appointed, the preachers of Rom. 10 are sent, and Andrew's obedience is initiated by Jesus' inquiry.) This means that such people are never their own; they live under orders. It also means that their assignment is crucial. Congregations need to hear both of these messages and the connection between them. God carries out his work by means of his appointed. There is no other way. Without watchmen there is no saving report (warning). Without the preached gospel there is no faith that saves. Without the "borne witness" there are no followers. When members of congregations proclaim, it makes a difference. Besides being a duty, it is something worth doing. This is an important word for a period in history when many people feel that there is nothing at all that is really worth doing or that will make any difference.

The difference made by proclamation depends, of course, on the power of God at work within it and through it. And here the essence of "not being their own" becomes clear. Confession is made by human lips out of human hearts, but the power of that profession to turn people (to save them) is God's. A good part of what this means is emphasized by both the Ezekiel and Romans passages. The success of the proclamation does not depend on the messenger. It is made quite clear to Ezekiel that his full responsibility is to be faithful to his duty ("If you warn the wicked, and he does not turn from his wickedness . . . he shall die . . . but you will have saved your life"). It is also clear in Romans 10 that the failure to believe belongs to Israel and not to those who had been sent. The question why some respond and some don't is not to burden the proclaimer into silence or into lack of enthusiasm, nor should the preacher waste time in and out of sermons trying to analyze or determine why some believe and some don't. (In particular he should avoid anti-Semitisms of any kind.)

The one message that is to be proclaimed by those sent is expressed in three somewhat different ways in the three texts. The central proclamation is that of the creedal formula, "Jesus is Lord" for "God raised him from the dead" (implied in Rom. 10:10 from v. 9). The meaning of that formula is elaborated by Ezekiel's message, which can easily be made christological—that is, God is at work in the lives of people (through Christ) to establish them as his own. This elaboration clarifies the creedal formula as a profession of what God is doing here and now, as well as a confession of what God did in the past in some other place. In the Gospel text, Andrew's words to Simon Peter ("We have found the Messiah") add the dimension of personal witness and the excitement with which the proclamation is made by the one who has experienced its truth. Both the Pauline text and the

Johannine text emphasize the dogmatic element of the proclamation. In a day when vague religious ideas are held strongly it may be important to emphasize that the word of those sent is never simply "I have faith" or "I believe." The proclamation is always a confession of faith *in*, that is, faith in God's activity in Christ.

The purpose of the proclamation is the saving of those who hear and believe. (In Ezekiel "saving" means to live rather than to die. In Romans it is connected in v. 12 to the "bestowal of riches," and in Joel 2:32, quoted in Rom. 10:13, it refers to those who "escape" and "survive." These words might well be used as graphic synonyms for "saved," allowing the texts themselves to define this key term.) This purpose of saving should be kept in mind and should qualify any warnings that must be given. The purpose of proclamation is not to condemn. "Wickedness" is to be pointed out, but only in order to show what God has done about it through Christ.

The audience for the proclamation emphasized in these texts is made up of people who have not yet heard the gospel. This outward thrust is present in the idea of "being sent." The watchman is not appointed to sit around and tell the king what he already knows. He is sent to get information and bring it back. The Christian proclaimer, on the other hand, is appointed to take his "information" and go with it. It is intended for the whole world. John the Baptist points Andrew to the One he has not yet seen, and Andrew tells his brother who has not yet heard. The church's task is incomplete without such outward movement and direction.

The emphasis on a personal and particular word in the Ezekiel text should not be taken as a critique of mass proclamation (of which the church does too little as it is). It should be used rather as a reminder that proclamation always occurs within a specific context (even mass media have their target areas and groups). "When you've seen one, you've seen them all" is true neither of audiences nor neighborhoods. A word that addresses needs in one place may be almost irrelevant in another. The emphasis on a personal and particular word in Ezekiel can also remind us that to proclaim a general word is not good enough (even in mass proclamation). No two "wickednesses" are exactly alike. No two people "turn from righteousness" in exactly the same way. The king may need a different word from the watchman than does the archer. In both cases, the emphasis in Ezekiel insists that in order to proclaim effectively, the preacher and congregation must be in contact. He must climb the tower (as a watchman) and see what's out beyond the wall. But more than that, he must go outside the wall. And there he must both listen and speak.

St. Thomas, Apostle

DECEMBER 21

Lutheran	Roman Catholic*	Episcopal
Judg. 6:36–40		Hab. 2:1–4
Eph. 4:11–16	Eph. 2:19–22	Heb. 10:35—11:1
John 14:1–7	John 20:24–29	John 20:24–29

While Thomas is only mentioned by name in the synoptic Gospels, he is individualized in John's Gospel. He is shown to be loyal (11:16), and also to be one who was slow to understand (14:5; 20:24–29). Loyalty and understanding come together in his confession which climaxes the Gospel.

The name Thomas is related to an Aramaic word meaning "twin." (In some versions the Greek word for "twin," *didymus,* is retained.) Tradition names Thomas as one of the five "Apostles of the East" and tells of his apostolic labors in Parthia (Persia) and in India. Neither the date nor cause of his death is known.

The day of St. Thomas was observed in the East from the sixth century. It was adopted at Rome in the ninth century. No reason is known for the date of December 21.

EXEGESIS

First Lesson: Judg. 6:36–40. This intriguing segment of Gideon's story is probably a piece of an account parallel to the narrative

*July 3

in 6:11b–17, or a variant of it. The segment is attributed to E (*Elohim,* v. 40; *ha-Elohim,* vv. 36 and 39).

Gideon has been called by God to "deliver Israel from the hand of Midian" (6:14), whose plundering raids have reduced Israel to cave dwellers in a wasted land. Gideon is most reluctant to accept the assignment. In the account of vv. 11b–17 he questions both assurances given to him by "the angel of the Lord." He shrugs off the angel's assurance that the Lord is with him by suggesting that the Lord's presence hasn't been doing him and his countrymen much good of late. Then he questions the accuracy of the angel's judgment that he is a "mighty man of valor": "My clan is the weakest in Manasseh, and I am the least in my family." In the account of vv. 36–40, Gideon puts God first through one test and then, cautiously, through another.

One of the charming aspects of this second account is in what happens between the first and second test. Gideon first asks that during the night God keep the ground (threshing floor) dry while covering a fleece of wool with dew. God meets the test, but Gideon suddenly realizes that the test he had devised wasn't foolproof. Overnight the fleece would naturally catch and retain moisture while the ground dew would evaporate quickly. So with "hat in hand," Gideon cautiously asks God to do it again, only in reverse order (keep the fleece dry and the ground wet). God obliges.

The most apparent connection between Gideon's story in Judg. 6:36–40 and that of Thomas in John's Gospel is the request for proof. Both men appear reluctant to believe a word that is incompatible with what they see and the conditions of their lives. Both are cautious about hurling themselves into a promise which is given without a supporting sign. In thinking about Thomas, it may be helpful to remember that Gideon's request for proof was not wholly inappropriate. It can be labeled as a lack of faith, but it may also have been seen as an act of prudence, or as the attempt by Gideon to clarify God's command to him. At least, it probably would not have seemed strange to any of Gideon's comrades.

Another connection between the stories of Gideon and Thomas may be seen in the persistence with which God (Jesus) holds to his

plan for them. Gideon's arguments and excuses bring only another
command and promise; both of his requests are met without rebuke.
There is no way either for Thomas to avoid the One who called him.

Second Lesson: Eph. 4:11–16. These verses defy precise and
clear exposition. Their purpose is not so much theological definition
as it is inspiration. The weighty language of v. 13 and the ill-coor-
dinated figures of vv. 14–16 particularly encourage this view. Rather
than explaining doctrinal matters the passage calls upon Christians to
love the church, respect its special ministries, and play out their full
part in its service.

The church is referred to here as the body of Christ, and a number
of special ministries are enumerated as Christ's gifts to that body.
These ministries do not exist for themselves. They have been given so
that all the people may be made fit for service. Thomas, of course, was
one of the gifts, an apostle (which group leads the list of special
ministries). One category that does not appear in a similar list in 1 Cor.
12:28 is that of evangelist. These evangelists may be seen as continuing the missionary work that the apostles once did (distinguished from
the work of pastors and teachers, which relates more to the internal
economy of the church).

The church is seen here as moving both within and toward unity.
Unity is a given (4:3) but it is also to be "attained" (4:13). Unity, and
the hymnic qualities which describe it (v. 13), are clearly connected to
the person of Christ. There is no unity apart from him. Within this
movement each person plays an essential role. The whole of chap. 4
points to the "grace given to each" (v. 7). This direction is supported
in v. 16 by the reference to "each part."

The church is constituted by interdependent parts (the "body"
image remains undeveloped). Each part shares in the life which
comes from Christ, and each part serves as a channel which passes on
the life it receives.

How one resolves certain tensions in this passage will probably
depend upon one's theological perspective. Whether one emphasizes
the church as a corporate unity or whether one rather stresses the
personal growth of individual Christians may well depend on one's

commitment to the visible unity of the church. Whether one understands the description in v. 13 to be that of Christ himself or rather that of the "saints" in him may depend on how one understands the function of grace. Whether one sees continuous growth (progression) for Christians toward their goal or rather sees the goal as parousial gift may depend on one's concept of eschatology. The passage has been used to support each of these several options.

Gospel: John 14:1–7. These verses constitute the opening words of Jesus' farewell discourse and prayer. They were probably selected for the day of St. Thomas, Apostle, because they include a brief dialogue between Thomas and Jesus, and because Thomas's question (v. 5) may well represent his general caution (and possibly his facility for misapprehension).

Jesus wants to reassure his troubled disciples that they will not be abandoned for long. He tells them that he will return after his "preparation" (his departure, death, resurrection, and ascension) and will take them into union with himself and with his Father (belief in Jesus and in God is the same thing—v. 1). This union has often been interpreted as occurring in the Parousia (either near or distant) or in the hour of death. It seems to be more in keeping with the Fourth Gospel, however, to view this union as that which occurs within the body of Christ (wherever the glorified Jesus is, there is the Father).

It is Thomas's question that enables, or forces, Jesus to explain how the union he promises is to be achieved. Thomas's lack of understanding (or caution) can be seen as helpful in the sense that it seemed to bring the truth out more clearly than it otherwise might have been. But his question may also exhibit foolishness, that is, he simply didn't know something he should have known. In either case, the question is an enabling one, and there is no rebuke for its being asked. (The words "if you had known me" in v. 7, which sound like a rebuke, seem meant for all the disciples rather than for Thomas alone, and they can be understood as a statement of fact as well as a statement contrary to fact.)

In response to Thomas's question, Jesus claims that he is the way to the Father (and that that is where he is going). The Father is the goal.

Jesus is the truth because he alone reveals the Father, and he is the life because he enables people to know that the Father is their goal. Jesus is the way because he is the truth through which comes life.

Jesus' answer to Thomas is not uncomplicated. Much has been written about the meaning of the three nouns "way," "truth," "life," and the relationship between them (the foregoing represents one interpretation). Some things, however, stand out very clearly. God the Father is not directly accessible; faith is attached to a revelation made in historical existence. Jesus does not need a way as do the disciples; he is the way. The words way, truth, and life describe Jesus in terms of his mission; they do not simply describe what he is, but rather they describe what he is for us. Life and truth are not at the disposal of people; Jesus alone is the way. Truth is not just learning; it is something lived and belonged to.

HOMILETICAL INTERPRETATION

A choice of theme for this day should depend in large part on what references to Thomas are planned for the Lenten and Easter seasons. The most significant Thomas passage (John 20:24–29) is assigned elsewhere. Nonetheless, there are some striking homiletical possibilities for this day that need not overlap with what may be said later in the church year.

One direction for homiletical development can highlight not only Thomas the disciple but also certain common aspects of Christian discipleship. Gideon asks for proof and Thomas asks for explanation. Both requests may stem either from faith or from lack of faith. Gideon, for example, may simply epitomize Israel's corrupt condition, and Thomas may represent the unbelief of the Jews. On the other hand, both Gideon and Thomas may be seen as men of faith who are seeking clarification, if not certainty. Neither choice should overlook the fact that both requests were tolerated and responded to. In the case of Thomas, moreover, it seems as though his question served as a catalyst, enabling Jesus to make his point more clearly and thus benefit all the disciples. One inference to be drawn from this is that whether or not particular questions are apparently useful, they should not be repressed. This is true for questions which seek instruction (there are no stupid questions). It is also true for expressions of doubt.

Doubt will not disappear until the eschaton, and it is good for us to recognize that fact in word and in deed.

Gideon caught himself in his own foolishness (and some might suggest that Thomas did also). He looks a little like the fairy-tale characters who make what they think is the first of three brilliant wishes only to discover that they wasted it by stupid calculation. Gideon, with some courage we imagine, presumed on God's patience by his first demand for proof only to discover that the test he devised proved nothing at all (beyond the fact that wool holds moisture). When he realized how badly he had calculated, he must have felt keenly the truth of his former excuse to the angel, "my clan is the weakest in Manasseh, and I am the least in my family" (6:15). And yet God called Gideon and tenaciously remained with him. It has been suggested that the choice of Gideon was made not only at random but almost as a deliberate attempt by God to show his own power by picking one who was weak. One could also conclude with Paul that once again God chose what was weak in the world "to shame the strong" (1 Cor. 1:27). In any case, Gideon well illustrates the way God has always worked in regard to his chosen ones. He selects for great tasks those who seem, even to themselves, to be incapable of mediocre ones. This is no less true of us than it was of Gideon (or of Thomas).

Both Gideon and Thomas are confronted by truth and are called upon to believe in it. Gideon is confronted by God's statement and asked to believe in its reliability, in the ability of God to perform what is required. Thomas is confronted by Jesus and asked to believe that he is the revelation of the Father (and the way to the Father). In the case of both men the truth is more than an idea to be accepted; it is something that must determine their existence. In truth Gideon must face the Midianites, and in truth Thomas must face the perplexities and abandonment of the crucifixion. Truth is not that to which one nods one's head, it is that to which one belongs. Truth appears, is responded to, and lived in within all the exigencies, the pressing necessities, of historical life.

A second homiletical direction is suggested mainly by the text from Ephesians. St. Thomas, Apostle, was one of Christ's gifts to the church, one of those who laid its very foundation (2:19-20). He was one specifically appointed to equip God's people for service. Regardless of what is made of his caution (or foolishness), Thomas is to be remembered with honor and thanksgiving.

The passage from Ephesians was written in a time when a ministerial office was developing within the church. A developed order with bishops and elders and deacons is not evident, but neither are the elements of a ministry of function as enumerated in 1 Cor. 12:28 (workers of miracles, healers, helpers). Special ministries exist within the church, and they should be recognized as such because they are the gift of Christ. But the gift of the ministries is not to those appointed to fill them. Those who fill the offices are rather a gift to the church. The offices do not exist in and of themselves. Their purpose is to "equip the saints," to animate the entire membership of Christ's body in the work he has given it. Neither anticlericalism nor clericalism is appropriate.

It is clear that ministry is not the exclusive calling of those appointed to special orders within the church's structure. Ministry is the calling of each member of the body. Church members can never be just consumers. Individuals cannot leave everything to the corporate whole. Each person must be an organically healthy, contributing part.

The story of Thomas makes clear that the central question for the church is always one concerning Christ. Thomas's own query quickly comes back in the form of another. Thomas says "Tell me," and Jesus says, "Believe in me." Thomas asks, "Will you explain?" and Jesus asks, "Will you follow?" The question is not so much whether we admit certain things about Jesus (his right, for example, to claim that he alone is the way because he is truth and life). The question is rather whether or not we will own the things we admit concerning Jesus, and whether or not we will confess those things by living them. It is not so much a matter of having a map as it is a matter of traveling on the basis of that map. The church is one when it makes common confession concerning Christ and not when it is of a single mind on all matters (doctrine, organization, liturgical expression). The church is one when that common confession is lived out both within the church and through it.

In a very real sense, of course, the church is one whether or not it makes and lives its confession. Christ is the head of the body, and it is from him that unity comes. A divided church does not mean a divided Christ. And yet the unity that is given must be increasingly appropriated. The church not only grows *from* Christ (Eph. 4:16), it also grows *into* him (4:15). It seeks to live out the fullness that it has been given.

The church lives out its confession when it recognizes (admits, owns, moves toward) all others who make the same confession. Divisions within and between congregations and denominations are always a scandal, a sign of incompleteness and deficiency. The church also lives out its confession when it holds firmly to that confession (v. 14) and when it does so in love (v. 15). Confessing Christ has both a doctrinal side and an ethical one. The Christian is not to be "tossed about" by error in either case. The church further lives out its confession when it seeks to build up not only itself but all people. Truth and love are to be lived not only within the confessing body. They are to be lived out in all human relationships.

St. Stephen, Deacon and Martyr

DECEMBER 26

Lutheran	Roman Catholic	Episcopal
2 Chron. 24:17–22		Jer. 26:1–9, 12–15
Acts 6:8—7:2a, 51–60	Acts 6:8–10; 7:54–59	Acts 6:8—7:2a; 51c–60
Matt. 23:34–39	Matt. 10:17–22	Matt. 23:34–39

Since the fourth century the days immediately after Christmas have been devoted to the "companions of Christ" *(comites Christi)*, members of his family and the early martyrs. Since the fifth or sixth centuries the Western church has focused on the martyrs rather than on the family members. It has followed Christmas with the three festivals of St. Stephen, St. John, and the Holy Innocents. Medieval commentators suggest that this triduum reveals a triple kind of martyrdom: St. Stephen, martyr in-will-and-deed; St. John, martyr in-will but not in-deed; the Holy Innocents, martyrs in-deed but not in-will.

The festival of St. Stephen honors him as the first Christian martyr (the "protomartyr"). He was one of the original seven deacons chosen to supervise the work of the Christian community in Jerusalem. He was later tried by the Sanhedrin and stoned to death (the full account is in Acts 6:1—8:2). It is possible that December 26 was the actual date of his martyrdom.

EXEGESIS

First Lesson: 2 Chron. 24:17–22. The reason for the choice of this lection for St. Stephen, Deacon and Martyr, is apparent. It reports the stoning of the prophet Zechariah, an event which is connected by the Gospel text to the martyrdom of early Christian missionaries (of which group Stephen was the first). The Zechariah mentioned in Matthew (23:35) is the same Zechariah referred to in 2 Chronicles, even though Matthew identifies him differently (Matthew was evidently confused). He was the son of Jehoiada, the chief priest of the temple at the time of King Ahaziah's death (2 Kings 11:4, among others).

The passage is part of the chronicler's theological interpretation of the reign of Ahaziah's son Joash, King of Judah. Its chief source is 2 Kings 12, or its parallel. It tells simply but strongly of the apostasy of Joash following the death of Jehoiada. Induced by "the princes of Judah," Joash turned from the temple and its cult (the "continual burnt offerings" noted in v. 14) and took up an earlier practice of idol worship. The worship of Asherah (the Hebrew equivalent for the Canaanite goddess Ashirtu or Ashratu) and the erection of sacred symbols of this goddess of fertility were strictly forbidden to the Israelites (see Exod. 34:13; Isa. 17:8; 27:9; Mic. 5:14). Joash's conversion seems complete; they "forsook the house of the Lord, the God of their fathers" (v. 18)

Joash is granted an exceptional chance to turn around once more. The prophet sent to testify against him is none other than the son of the chief priest to whom he owed so much. The "kindness" referred to in v. 22 is constituted by far more than simple favors. According to 2 Chron. 22:10—23:3, Jehoiada and his wife were instrumental in saving Joash's infant life and in placing him on the throne. But Joash did not listen to Jehoiada's son. Far from it! Inflamed by the "conspiracy" of the people, he ordered Zechariah to be killed by stoning.

Joash's crime against Zechariah did not go unpunished. The "avenging" for which Zechariah cries with his last breath comes quickly. The chronicler reports that Joash is severely wounded by invading Syrians (not in keeping with the Deuteronomist's account in Kings) and then murdered by some of his officers (here Kings agrees). According to the chronicler, Joash's punishment extends even beyond his death: he is not buried in the cemetery of the kings (here again Kings disagrees).

Chiefly evidenced in this interpretive passage is the chronicler's doctrine of retribution. At points he has manipulated history in the interests of his teaching; that is, divine punishment follows immediately upon the act of wrongdoing. Yet he tells a good story. And his purpose is hardly to distort. He is convinced that God will intervene directly and immediately in all human affairs. That is the truth he wishes to impress upon his readers.

Second Lesson: Acts 6:8—7:2a, 51–60. This lection contains almost all the essential elements of Stephen's story. Only the account of his appointment, the major part of his sermon before the council, and Luke's note (8:1) that Saul "was consenting to his death" (later affirmed by Paul in Acts 22:20) are not included. The omission of these items in no way destroys the dramatic flow of the narrative. Indeed, to include them would be a disruptive alternative.

For whatever reason, it seems clear that Stephen's activity was not limited to that specified by his appointment, that is, to supervise the work of the Christian community in Jerusalem. The text indicates that he "did great wonders and signs," and his sermon before the council suggests that he was not a stranger to preaching. Angered by his "wonders and signs," or by his preaching, or by the fact that they could never better him in a dispute, a seemingly large number of Hellenistic Jews had Stephen arrested and tried before the Sanhedrin on the basis of allegations made by "false witnesses." Exactly who arrested Stephen and on what authority is not clear. He was accused, however, of continually blaspheming both Moses and God (vv. 13–14).

Stephen's address to the council (7:2–50) is more of a sermon than it is a legal defense (it is the kind of survey of Israel's history that belongs to the Christian kerygma). Stephen's concluding words (7:51–53), which are not really prepared for by what precedes them, are a stinging accusation which infuriates his accusers and judges. He answers their ensuing rage with what is for them further blasphemy (vv. 55–56). In a kind of uncontrollable anger, and without verbal judgment, "they" (the councillors or the witnesses—Deut. 17:1–7— or both) drag Stephen out of the city (good Levitical law—Lev. 24:11ff.; Num. 15:35) and stone him.

Throughout the event, as in his ministry (v. 8), Stephen is empowered by the Holy Spirit (v. 55), which is itself a fulfillment of Jesus' promise recorded in Luke 21:15. Perhaps it is the Spirit's presence which enables Stephen to be so Jesus-like in attitude and response. (Perhaps Luke had Jesus' own trial and death in mind when he wrote of this first Christian martyrdom.) Stephen's words in vv. 56, 59, and 60 closely resemble Jesus' words in Luke 22:69; 23:46; and 23:34. His dying prayer is much different from that of the prophet Zechariah who was killed at the command of Joash (2 Chron. 24).

Gospel: Matt. 23:34–39. This passage consists of two sections that may not have been originally connected. The first, vv. 34–36, is congruous with an OT "oracle of disaster" such as often follows a series of woes (Isa. 5:18–24). The second, vv. 37–39, is a lament. Both sections correspond to passages in Luke's Gospel. Vv. 34–36 correspond to Luke 11:49–51. Vv. 37–39 correspond to Luke 13:34–35. In both Lucan passages the words which Matthew ascribes to Jesus were spoken by Wisdom (stated in Luke 11:49, and appropriate to Luke 13:34–35).

The two sections of this lection are connected by repeated reference to the killing of the prophets and others sent by God. All the martyrs in the OT are summed up in Abel and Zechariah, the first and the last (2 Chronicles, where Zechariah's death is reported, is the last book in the Hebrew OT). All Christian martyrs, of whom Stephen was the first, are included in the "prophets and wise men and scribes" of v. 34. Jesus himself is included if v. 36 is understood to mean that he is the final messenger, one who will suffer a kind of summary of the fates of all the rest. The "killing of the prophets" also reflects the situation of Matthew's own community. V. 34 describes a time when the church had been forced to separate from the Jewish community ("*your* synagogues"). It describes a time when the church had to look out for its own life, when Christians were pursued from city to city and when the risk of martyrdom ran high.

The most immediate referent for the coming upon Israel of "all the righteous blood shed on earth" is the destruction of Jerusalem and the temple in A.D. 70 (see 24:2). Another referent appears in v. 38. This verse can be understood to mean that when Jesus left the temple on that day (24:1) the temple was emptied of God. The intimate relation between God and Israel was ended. V. 39 suggests that the Jews will not see their Messiah until they accept Christianity. There is the further inference that God's mission through the church is no longer to Israel per se but to the Gentiles.

What is so lamentable is that none of this had to happen. The sending of prophets and missionaries by God (Jesus) was meant to be a gathering of his people. It was an offer of protection, refuge, and sustenance (the "hen" image of v. 37) which came not once but many times. It was an offer continuously rejected by those who refused to break with the past by way of repentance and submission to the will of God. That refusal need not have occurred.

HOMILETICAL INTERPRETATION

Three homiletical possibilities suggest themselves for this day and its lessons. They have to do with martyrdom, its cause, and its veneration.

The word *martus* ("witness") originally referred both to a legal witness and to any witness to facts. In Christian usage it was first applied to the contents of the gospel proclamation. A *martus* was one who witnessed to Christ by word and life. By the middle of the second century, the term reached its full development. It came to designate those who actually shed their blood in bearing witness. In this regard, it's interesting to note that the church distinguished between "martyrs" and "confessors." Confessors were those who had been exiled or otherwise punished for their witness but who had not been killed. Stephen, therefore, was a martyr in the fullest sense of the word. And the account of his trial and death fills out particular dimensions of that word's richest meaning.

The last three statements of Stephen before his accusers are almost identical with three statements of Jesus during his trial and death. In whatever way this similarity is explained (presence of the Spirit, Luke's authorship), the fact that it is there suggests the close identification of Stephen with the crucified Christ. He is seen to be within the closest fellowship of Christ's sufferings. When Stephen was exposed to public insult, when he suffered and died as a witness, "Christ took a visible form in his church" (Bonhoeffer). There is no discipleship more loyal and complete than this.

The power of Christ's suffering was at work in Stephen's martyrdom. In no sense was Stephen's life wasted. His trial enabled him to preach in a place and to people perhaps otherwise inaccessible. It may well have been his beatific death that worked on an approving Saul (Acts 8:1 and 22:20) and readied him for conversion. Tertullian *(Apologeticum)* first noted that "the blood of the martyrs is the seed of the church." Stephen's suffering and death were supposed to cut off his witness (so that his accusers could unstop their ears—Acts 7:57), but they only pushed his testimony forward.

The fruits of Christ's passion were also at work in Stephen's martyrdom. While Stephen certainly did not atone for the sins of his accusers, he surely bore them. He bore them as a scapegoat might (Zechariah also did this). Transferred to him was all the anger, rage, and blind passion of his enemies (as if when he is finally driven out into the wilderness their guilt will be gone). But he did not bear the sins of his enemies only by accepting their full consequence. He bore them also by overcoming them. He not only suffered their sins; he forgave them. (This Zechariah did not do.) Stephen did not allow the alienation which sin causes to occur. He refused to be in any kind of relationship to these people other than the one he was in before their offense was committed. He allowed no barrier of enmity to be raised.

Clearly there is peace for Stephen in his complete discipleship. He is "in Christ" in joy as well as in suffering. The "Lord Jesus" (7:59) transfigured Stephen's final hour. "His face was like the face of an angel"; he "saw the glory of God"; he "fell asleep." Stephen bore the cross and triumphed.

Stephen was only the first of the martyrs. Historical records give us a very incomplete list of the others. Also hidden are those in our own day whose Christian discipleship is carried to the fullest measure. They are all special people, those to whom the grace of martyrdom is given. But the fact of their presence among us should not blind us to the fact that each of us also is called to witness. Our *martus* may never include the shedding of our blood, but it is nonetheless connected to both the sufferings and the triumph of Christ. In Christ, we are to bear the sins of others, accepting the consequences of those sins but refusing to allow them to cause separation. In Christ, we are to forgive our "enemies." In Christ, this is the cross through which our peace comes.

It is clear from our texts that the blood of the martyrs cannot be shed, nor God's messengers rejected, with impunity. Joash had no excuse for his violent judgment against Zechariah the prophet. Joash was shamed in battle, slain without capability of defending himself, and buried in disgrace. The scribes and the Pharisees had no excuse for their savage treatment of prophets, Christian missionaries, and Jesus. Their temple was destroyed and they were forsaken by God—what they had was taken away and given to someone else. There is particular bite in these dramas because of Jesus' intimation in Matt. 23:30 that any present performance is no better than that of the past. Each generation is in danger of rejecting those whom God sends. Violence is never far under the surface.

While the intensity of the rage which erupts upon God's messengers cannot be fully explained, there are some signs as to its cause. Zechariah challenged the values by which Joash decided to live. More specifically, Zechariah told the king how it was with him, that he lived in the darkness of falsehood and perversity, that he was not the center of his world. Christian missionaries (and Stephen) told Israel that their perfect discipline amounted to nothing, that God had something new to say that demanded their letting go of the past by means of repentance. It doesn't really matter here that it is Joash and Israel. God's coming to anyone is always disruptive, a challenge to every idolatry, chiefly the idolatries of the self and of the past, and the values used to support them. From such disruption springs either submission or attack.

We are invited by these texts to see the disaster that follows rejection and bloodletting as God's response. We will not want to adopt the chronicler's doctrine of divine retribution, but we are encouraged to accept the fact that God intervenes in judgment between the deed and its outcome. In neither of the cases mentioned, however, is the judgment final. Joash dies but Judah continues. Israel is left desolate but the gospel is still proclaimed within it (though not exclusively). The offer of protection, refuge, and sustenance continues.

Surely one of the reasons why we commemorate the martyrs is because of their "unsurpassable devotion" (Polycarp) to Christ and because of the motivating power of their witness to us. They are examples to be imitated. But they are not only that. They, like us, are also justified sinners, and thus they are representatives of the grace of God in which we all participate. Above everything else, their lives show us the gifts which God confers upon all of us through Christ.

And so we commemorate them also because they call us to a greater confidence in those gifts of grace. Finally, when we commemorate the martyrs we give thanks that they and we are members of the same body, that these *comites Christi* are our brothers and sisters in Christ.

St. John, Apostle and Evangelist

DECEMBER 27

Lutheran	Roman Catholic	Episcopal
Gen. 1:1–5, 26–31		Exod. 33:18–23
1 John 1:1—2:2	1 John 1:1–4	1 John 1:1–9
John 21:20–25	John 20:2–8	John 21:19b–24

This day focuses on the Apostle John and on the author of the Fourth Gospel. It is uncertain, however, whether or not they are the same person. Their identification has often been assumed, but biblical scholars have raised serious questions about that assumption. In any case, the evangelist and the apostle do share a common tradition. That is, the apostle is the source of the historical tradition that has come into the Gospel, whether or not he actually wrote it. It is this Johannine tradition and those who embodied it that are commemorated on this day.

John the Apostle, along with his brother James, and Peter, was chosen by Jesus to share in special experiences. He is thought to have been "the disciple whom Jesus loved" mentioned repeatedly in the Fourth Gospel. Tradition has it that he died at an advanced age (94–100 years) in Ephesus following a period of exile on a lonely island in the Greek Archipelago. He is the only one of the twelve apostles who is supposed to have died of natural causes. Hence, a "martyr," but in-will rather than in-deed.

As early as the fourth century in the East James and John were both commemorated on December 27. John appears alone when the festival was accepted at Rome in the sixth century.

EXEGESIS

First Lesson: Gen. 1:1–5, 26–31. This lection is from the priestly (P) literary tradition (postexilic, ca. 538–450 B.C.). Its central purpose is neither to speculate nor to inspire awe. It is a credo, a carefully written story based on centuries of reflection. Each detail is important. The central question about the text is not so much whether it is true or not. The main question rather has to do with its meaning.

It is important to remember that the first eleven chapters of Genesis serve as an introduction to that history which begins with the call of Abraham in chap. 12. These verses are not primarily intended as a call to faith in creation (or as a doctrine of creation). They are basically a preface to something else. They are meant to relate the construction of the cosmos to the redemption of Israel. Yahweh who "made covenant" is the Creator of the world. The call here is to faith in salvation.

The fact that creation occurs by God's word emphasizes the distinction between the Creator and that which is created. The creation is the product of God's will rather than just an efflux or reflection of his being. It is the means by which God relates to the world without becoming tied to its order. Creation by word also emphasizes the fact that the whole world belongs to God. The world came into being by virtue of God's personal command, and it will always be capable of influence by his word.

God first created light. Then he separated light and darkness and gave them names. Even light, without which it seems impossible to conceive of creation, is created. It is ordered, placed, designated. So also is darkness. A part of the original chaos, night, remains, but it is limited and stabilized. The alternation of day and night, light and darkness, is a constant reminder that chaos is held in check only by God's creative power. The continued life of all created things rests wholly upon God.

In regard to the creation of man and woman, "image" refers more to task than it does to gift. Human beings are God's representatives in the task of "dominion" (v. 28 suggests that this means to replenish, "fill," as well as to "subdue"). Even though human life is creation's climax, men and women are still creatures. They are related primarily to God and are dependent upon him for both life and purpose.

Second Lesson: 1 John 1:1—2:2. The author of this epistle may not have been the author of the Fourth Gospel, but it seems probable that he was at least influenced by it. It is also probable that this lection includes three insertions added by an "ecclesiastical redactor" (1:7b, 9; 2:2).

First John is an epistle of affirmation. The author seeks to assure the faithful in his community that they possess the true Christianity. He does this over against the real threat of Gnostic influence and schism. Some of the troublesome heretical claims are clearly voiced and responded to in 1:8, 10 ("no sin") and in 1:6 (ethics don't really matter). Vv. 1–2 of chap. 1 are also a response to a central Gnostic claim that Jesus Christ did not "come in the flesh" (4:2).

The author does not assert that he was an eyewitness to "the life made manifest" (1:2). He writes of "seeing" and "touching," but such words probably refer to the mediating power of proclamation (the tradition) rather than to physical perception. He is therefore proclaiming what the faithful had also seen and touched.

The statement that "God is light" is a highly suggestive one. It has been understood to refer both to the nature of God (for example, it is his nature to reveal himself) and to the meaning that God has for human life (for example, providing the illumination necessary to find one's way). In this passage it carries a moral connotation and defines both God's nature (God is without taint of evil) and the mode in which

God's people are to work (in light rather than in darkness). This mode is clearly an ethical one. Light has a demanding, imperative character (cf. 2:3–5). Truth (v. 6) is something done.

The word "fellowship" expresses a central reality for the author (indeed, 1:3 claims it as the goal). It describes a union in common faith brought about by the proclamation (the legitimate tradition). It is a union with "the Father and with his Son Jesus Christ." It is also a union of Christians in which each is so close and vital that life itself depends upon it. Its gift is joy. The fact that one must continue to walk is a sign of the union's incompleteness. But it is nonetheless real.

In some ways vv. 10ff. are particularly interesting. Every attempt to sculpt a Christianity without sin is condemned. To deny sin would be to claim that God made a wrong diagnosis. It would be to deny God as the forgiving one. That would be a rejection of God's word as his word. While the author thus insists on the reality of forgiveness, he does not want his readers to misunderstand. Sin must be taken seriously (2:2).

Gospel: John 21:20–25. This lection was selected for use on this day because of its reference to the fate and standing of the "disciple whom Jesus loved" (identified by tradition with the Apostle John). Johannine authorship of the Fourth Gospel is certainly disputed. Arguments are strong that this passage is the work of a later redactor who is to be distinguished from the unknown author of this Gospel. But there are major disagreements as to the redactor's source. It is possible that the passage represents an original composition by the redactor. It is also possible that it is built upon an existing source. The passage itself seems to be part of an appendix to the Fourth Gospel, which probably ended at 20:31. The purpose of the appendix is also disputed: the question of ecclesiastical authority, the nature of discipleship ("following"), and so forth.

V. 23 indicates that the Beloved Disciple (John) has died and that this may have caused some problems for those who understood that he was to live until the Parousia (implied by v. 22). The words of v. 23 correct that misunderstanding, and vv. 20–23 expand the context. The author indicates that the disciple's death was not an error. His death was not premature, nor was his natural death (old age) of less significance than that of Peter (martyrdom). Each man had a different destiny, but both were part of Jesus' plan and both gave glory to God.

The statement in v. 24 seeks to authenticate the truth of what has been written. Its exact meaning is unclear. It seems to claim "eyewitness" authority, but that may not be the case. Indeed, it need not be the case. According to the Fourth Gospel, authenticity does not depend simply on eyewitnesses. The "Spirit of truth" also bears witness (15:26). He bears witness through the entire Gospel regardless of the fact that it is both memory and reflection (and regardless of its authorship). The "disciple" in v. 24 may be the redactor, and the "we" in v. 24 may be his community. Neither were eyewitnesses, but their testimony is still true.

The word "brethren" in v. 23 is of special interest. The Greek *adelphos* is overwhelmingly the term used in the NT to designate Christians. It is their universal, standard name. Begotten as God's children through the gift of the Spirit, Christians become the brothers (and sisters) of Jesus and of one another.

HOMILETICAL INTERPRETATION

The texts for this day are somewhat kaleidoscopic. Each one contains multiple themes, and there seems to be an almost endless variety of homiletic possibilities offered by their connection. However, certain themes seem more appropriate than others for a day commemorating the Johannine tradition (and the apostle who is its source). Some of these themes are suggested by what follows.

The tradition of John the Apostle reminds us that not all followers of Jesus have the same destiny or the same demands made upon their lives. There seems to have been some embarrassment that John died of natural causes while all the other apostles died as martyrs. This embarrassment may be reflected in the medieval designation of John as a martyr in will rather than deed (he would have gladly shed his blood if the occasion had demanded it!). John was a martyr insofar as he was exiled, but he was still the only apostle who died nonviolently. Yet his witness was not less, nor was he of less importance than the others. The evangelist (redactor, John 21:20–25) urges us to see that both configurations are within the plan of Christ and both give him glory. Quiet, sustained witness is also the "seed of the church."

The apostle's witness is not weakened by his quiet death. Neither is the authenticity of the Johannine proclamation weakened because of its derivative-adoptive nature. More than likely, both the Fourth Gospel and the Johannine epistles were written by someone other than the eyewitness apostle. Even if they are based on a source stemming from the apostle, these writings are adaptations of received tradition. They include both memory and reflection. Nonetheless they form a reliable witness. The "Spirit of truth" is at work in both the source and the adaptation. We can therefore trust what we have before us in these texts (and elsewhere in the Scriptures). We are urged to stay within their proclamation, even as we adopt what we have received in them for a new time and place. "That which we have seen and heard we proclaim also to you" (1 John 1:3). Both aspects of that event—Scripture tradition and our preaching—carry a guarantee of reliability.

It was noted that creation by word (Genesis 1) emphasizes the distinction between the Creator and the creature. The narrative clearly bears the marks of the priestly tradition. The God who emerges from the story is a God of pattern and of hierarchy. (The universe has order and so does human life; by analogy, it must depend on ritual, ceremony, tradition.) God is a majestic being who inspires awe. He communicates himself but he is distant, exalted, transcendent. As the notion of a creative word was further developed in Judaism, the emerging picture of God also changed. Now it is through intermediaries that God communicates himself and establishes his relationship with the world and its people. But it was finally in the Johannine tradition that the creative word reached its fullest content. The word becomes flesh in Jesus of Nazareth, and God's self-communication is total. The word is now not only heard but it is also seen and touched. In Jesus the purpose of God's self-communication from the beginning becomes clear: that "you may have fellowship with us; and our fellowship is with the Father and with his Son Jesus Christ" (1 John 1:3). The distinction between Creator and creature remains, but the Creator's revelation of himself is complete, and union with him is possible through this word made flesh. The God who makes covenant with us through his Son is the Creator of the world. The creation story is itself a call to faith in our salvation.

The author of 1 John urges all true believers to "walk in the light." That phrase and its context suggest several aspects of Christian living.

The light in which Christians are to walk is God. Whether we think of God as light itself or think of him as the Creator of light makes little difference in this context. In either case, the light is not something generated by us. It is given, and we are dependent upon it. We must relate to it but can in no way possess it. Our posture is that of the creature. If "God is light" is understood in its moral connotation (as 1 John invites us to do), we may sense something of our situation in relation to God's commandments (2:4–6). They are given. We cannot alter them. We must relate to them either by walking in them or by not walking in them—there is no third choice.

The light is not something that we have on a permanent basis. It is something in which we must walk continuously. Light is a gift which must be acted upon. Its whole purpose is to illuminate our world so that we can move about safely and joyfully. As light, God's commandments continually expose new facts and features not seen before, or those hidden in shadows. They constantly reveal those places where creation is in danger of sinking into chaos, where nonbeing threatens that which God has called forth. They regularly illumine our lives so that we can move, become, engage one another, in safety and in joy. They are a continually acting gift to be acted upon.

To walk in the light of the commandments is to obey them. But it is also to acknowledge the darkness which they expose. The Johannine tradition knows of no life, no Christianity, without sin. To say that we are "beyond sin" or that we "do not sin" is a deception, a lie which makes God a liar (because he says we do sin). We are to acknowledge our darkness by confessing it, assured that our "advocate" will plead on our behalf (the ecclesiastical redactor of v. 9 makes the assurance remarkably clear). Thus both obedience and confession are essential parts of Christian living.

One cannot take the Johannine tradition seriously and still retain a shallow understanding of the church as a fellowship. The church is not simply a voluntary association. It is a union brought about by the action of God through proclamation. This union is not peripheral (an avocational hobby). Its centrality is declared by the fact that each of its members is given new status as a brother/sister of Christ ("brethren") and of one another. The church's life is not adequately described as one of mutual interest. It is rather a life of common faith, a life fed from a source beyond itself. Congeniality between persons with mutual interest is not the primary behavior of the church's people. Its members rather relate to each other in love (see 1 John 3:16–18). The church is not complete even when it has location and organization and program. It continues to "walk." The church does not determine its own agenda, nor does it measure its own success. It lives in obedience and in confession.

The Holy Innocents, Martyrs

DECEMBER 28

Lutheran	Roman Catholic	Episcopal
Jer. 31:15–17		Jer. 31:15–17
1 Pet. 4:12–19	1 John 1:5—2:2	Rev. 21:1–7
Matt. 2:13–18	Matt. 2:13–18	Matt. 2:13–18

This commemoration completes the post-Christmas triduum. It rounds out the triple theme of martyrdom by honoring the children of Bethlehem who were slaughtered by Herod in his futile attempt to kill the infant Jesus (Matt. 2:13–18). The innocent victims are seen as martyrs in-deed though not in-will.

It is possible that this festival was first held as early as the fourth century in the East. By the end of the fifth century it was observed throughout the Western church.

Since it is not at all certain that the commemorated slaughter ever occurred, the focus of this festival has often been on children in general or on all innocent victims.

EXEGESIS

First Lesson: Jer. 31:15–17. Chaps. 30—33 of Jeremiah are frequently called "the book of consolation." They are held to be a collection of the prophet's sayings which are of a hopeful nature, and they are thought to comprise a unit which develops the theme laid down in 30:3: "I will restore the fortunes of my people, Israel and Judah, . . . and I will bring them back to the land which I gave to their fathers." This theme is clearly present in the lectionary text.

The Jeremiah text was chosen to be read on this day because of its obvious connection with the Gospel. The evangelist Matthew quotes Jer. 31:15 in his story of the innocents' slaughter by Herod. Indeed, he points to the slaughter as a fulfillment of the prophet's words. While the authorship of many of the sayings in the book of consolation is in doubt, there seems to be general agreement that 31:15–17 was authored by Jeremiah.

Rachel was the mother of Joseph and Benjamin (Gen. 30:22 and 35:16–20) and thus was the ancestress of the tribes of Ephraim, Manasseh, and Benjamin. Ramah was near her burial place in the territory of Benjamin (1 Sam. 10:2) some five miles north of Jerusalem. In this text Rachel is pictured as weeping disconsolately for her exiled children. It could be that Jeremiah imagined that the spirit of Rachel haunted her tomb (a folk concept) or that in imagination he heard her weeping. It could also be that the prophet has voiced through Rachel his own grief (Jeremiah came from Anathoth, a village belonging to the tribe of Benjamin).

It is not clear whether these words belong to Jeremiah's early or late career. What exiles wept for (v. 15) and the hope given (vv. 16–17) are thus not clearly identifiable. If the words are early, they likely refer to those Israelites settled in distant places following the Assyrian victory in 721 b.c. The hope expressed is for the restoration of the nation, perhaps associated with the expansionist policy of the reforming Josiah. If the words are late, they likely refer to the whole of Israel, particularly the exiles of both 721 and 598. In this case the hope extended may be that of the new covenant (31:31–34).

Rachel is told that her work will be rewarded by the return of the exiled. Everything she did in bearing, raising, sorrowing, and interceding will not go unheard or unanswered. If Rachel's weeping is somehow that of the prophet, then perhaps her "work" is also. Rachel's intercession is Jeremiah's own, and the prophet here expresses the hope which gave heart to his task. In a situation emptied of all reason to hope he believed and proclaimed a new age of salvation. God will answer the cries of his faithful people.

Second Lesson: 1 Pet. 4:12–19. The situation addressed by this text has been described in different ways. One interpretation pictures a time of general persecution in which it was a governmental offense to be a Christian. Another interpretation assumes the more normal circumstance of hostility toward Christians living in an unfriendly environment. Since both interpretations can be supported, a decision may well depend on how strongly one wishes to move with the liturgical tradition of martyrdom. A situation of persecution certainly seems to be more in accord with a celebration of the Holy Innocents.

It has been suggested that vv. 12–16 are strikingly similar to Pliny's account of the persecution which occurred under Trajan (A.D. 98–117). The reference to "Christian" in v. 16 is taken as the actual ground of accusation. "Reproach" (v. 14) echoes the cries of angry mobs. "Murderer . . . thief . . . wrongdoer . . ." (v. 15) indicate that Christians were being tried as criminals and that the time was long past when a "defense" or "good behavior" would be of any help (3:15–16). Days of more normal abuse (suspicion, occasional local brutality) in no way prepared the Christian community for such an acute crisis. They were "surprised," shocked; "something strange" and unbelievable had come upon them (v. 12).

Whether or not the actual circumstance was one of severe persecution, the response of the author is the same. What is occurring is the beginning of the End, and it is natural that "the household of God" is the first to experience judgment (v. 17; Jer. 25:29; Ezek. 9:6; Mal. 3:1–6). Whether the judgment is a test, or a vehicle of separation, or a chance for the wayward to return, it is an opportunity for Christians to share in Christ's sufferings (v. 13). Such sharing brings joy through the experience of oneness with Christ. It is an occasion for blessing because of the Spirit's powerful presence (v. 14; Matt. 10:19–20; Acts 7:55). Christians undergoing such judgment-opportunity are simply to commit themselves to the care of their faithful Creator and continue loving and doing good (even though neither the commitment nor the service will stop the persecution-judgment).

While the author of 1 Peter is a Paulinist (shows dependence on Paul), the Spirit of v. 14 is more a visitor than a resident (the indwelling Spirit of Pauline thought). He accompanies the testimony of faith. He is bestowed on the persecuted, on Christians in the time of their suffering for the name of Christ (v. 14).

The author applies Prov. 11:31 (from the Septuagint) eschatologically. In the End (of which the persecution is the beginning) the disobedient will face a disaster unimaginable even to those suffering persecution. This fact might well give additional courage to Christians in their present plight. It might also warn them that escape by apostasy is no escape.

Gospel: Matt. 2:13–18. Given the cruelty of Herod and the enmity that surrounded Jesus almost from the beginning, a slaughter of children at Bethlehem seems possible enough. But the arguments against its historicity are too strong. There is no remembrance of the event later in Jesus' ministry; the massacre and flight are contradictory to Luke's record; there is no mention of such an event in secular accounts. Nonetheless, the slaughter of innocents could have happened—and has happened repeatedly in world history. Neither we nor Matthew's readers find such a vicious act difficult to imagine.

The evangelist's attention in this lection is on Jesus. Its details point to his uniqueness as the Son of God. It is suggested, for example, that the quotations from Hos. 11:1 (v. 15b) and Jer. 31:15 (v. 18) were most carefully chosen. Originally the Hosea passage referred to the exodus of Israel from Egypt. The widest reference of the Jeremiah text are the exiles to both Assyria and Babylon. Included in these quotations therefore are the two greatest trials of God's people and the two greatest demonstrations of God's power. In his flight (his exile) and in his return Jesus thus relived both moments of his nation's history and of God's salvation. He surpasses even Moses, whose own life involved massacre, flight, exile, and return.

Again, the lection indicates that Jesus was God's Son from the very beginning. The pattern here is the pattern of his ministry. He is forced to wander in insecurity (Matt. 8:20). He faces rejection by the populace and attack by leaders (Matt. 11:2—12:50). He is guided by God, in accordance with whose will his life is lived (and he is brought back from the exile of death by the power of God). Along the way there are some faithful Jews who, like his father and mother, surround him and, on occasion, defy the authorities in his service.

Still again, Jesus' flight points to his humility—and humiliation— before the powers of the world. There is a great discrepancy between King Herod and the King of the Jews. One rises with his armies and shows his fearful strength. The other flees. Yet while Herod fumes and sputters and is finally frustrated, Jesus sleeps peacefully in refuge. Control is not with Herod; it is with Jesus. The plan of God is to be fulfilled in him (Matt. 26:53–54).

Two additional notes may be helpful. Matthew here identifies Ramah (v. 18) with Bethlehem. It is a mistaken identification. Gen. 35:16–19 locates the site between Bethel and Ephrath. Here Ephrath is identified with Bethlehem, confusing Ephrath, the clan name, with the Benjamite place name. Again, the reference to Joseph's dream may reflect the fact that Matthew's story is based on a pre-Matthean Moses story connected to the dreams of the patriarch Joseph.

HOMILETICAL INTERPRETATION

The main source for a sermon on this day will probably be the lection from Matthew. Of least use as a source is the passage from Jeremiah. Some possibilities follow.

The designation of the Bethlehem children as martyrs in-deed but not in-will is an appropriate one. Their situation was different from that of the exiles in Jeremiah or that of the Christians in 1 Peter. The exiles had been part of a disobedient people. The Christians were part of a confessing church. The children just happened to be born in the wrong place at the wrong time. They had made decisions about nothing. They had made no confession. They were victims, caught between the unfolding plan of God and the angry resistance of the world's powerful. They were the first innocent casualties in a war between two kingdoms.

In the Matthew story, Bethlehem itself was a casualty. The Christmas texts encourage us to picture Bethlehem as a kind of Palestinian Camelot. The crowded inn (Luke) was more than balanced by the watching angels (Luke), the adoring magi, the brilliant star, and the believing shepherds (Luke). Then Herod spoke and the angel chorus became the inconsolable wailing of men and women (echoing the cries of the abandoned for centuries). The seemingly unassailable dream broke up. Beloved Bethlehem was shattered, and twenty or thirty babies were dead in the street. Bethlehem too had been caught in the middle. Resistance to the gospel is real. (It is said that because there are no secular records of this tragedy it probably never happened. It's intriguing to think that maybe the tragedy did happen but that it was not recorded because no one really cared. In any age of "cheap life," a few Bethlehems and a few infants are totally expendable, especially if they happen to be in the way of world powers determined to protect themselves.)

The death of the innocent children made a difference not only for Bethlehem but also for Jesus. The evangelist Matthew is concerned about demonstrating the uniqueness of Jesus, and he does so in the ways outlined in the exegetical section. But this massacre text also points dramatically to the common lot Jesus shared with his people ("'Emmanuel' [which means, God with us]"—Matt. 1:23). He is clearly a human being in relationship. Who he is and what he does (or promises) affects others; Mary and Joseph seek refuge, and the children are murdered because of him. He is also affected by the actions of other people; he is humbled and forced to flee by the threat of Herod. Again, Jesus is clearly at one with the oppressed. Later he becomes a poor carpenter in a poor country among oppressed people. But here already that oppression is made a part of his life. He is identified with it not only by his lowly birth but also by the death of twenty or thirty children at the grasping hand of the oppressor Herod. Still again, Jesus is supported by the investment of others in him. Now it is not simply the investment of Mary and Joseph—it is also the investment of lifeblood by Bethlehem's young. If Jesus is special, it must be in part because of the gift given to him by so many others.

If Jesus is somehow special because of the Bethlehem children, then it surely must also be said that the children are special because of him. Any child is special, and these special children might have died anyway. Herod was an assassin ("better to be a pig than Herod's son," it was said). He killed court officers, Jerusalem notables, and even three of his own sons. His sick wrath could have been unleashed at any time quite apart from Jesus. But these children were killed because of Jesus' birth, and while they can be listed simply as victims, the church counts them among the redeemed, the firstfruits, the followers of the Lamb (Rev. 14:1–5). In some premature way they shared in Christ's sufferings (1 Pet. 4:13). Through his later death for them (they were murdered but saved, while he was saved but murdered) they were given victory. They were part of the "brotherhood," called to "eternal glory in Christ," restored, established, and strengthened by the "God of all grace" (1 Pet. 5:9–10).

Jesus took the suffering and death of the Bethlehem children into himself. And he took the anguish and desolation of all the world's Rachels into himself. He is the Holy Innocent One murdered by all the accumulated resistance to God's kingdom. There has probably never been a day in history when at least one member of Christ's body has not bled. Their blood is the blood of Christ. Someone has said that there is only an eternal "now," in which the bleeding of Jesus is as actual today as it was two thousand years ago. The bleeding of all martyrs from before the time of Jesus and through all the centuries belongs to that eternal moment.

Much use has been made of 1 Peter in sermons to provide some rationale for the mystery of suffering. It is said, for example, that suffering tests, strengthens, confirms, and develops character. Suffering is turned to beauty and grace, it is said, by the controlling and connecting operation of the Spirit of glory. Many such sermons are powerful testimonies of faith and are pastorally helpful to anguished people. They seem to miss, however, both the eschatological thrust of the Petrine text and the fact that the suffering which is "for the name of Christ" is here specified (whether the situation is one of general persecution or one of more normal harassment). It seems somewhat illegitimate therefore to use the passage per se to speak about human suffering in general (or even about general human suffering as seen from the vantage point of Christian faith).

There is one item in the Petrine text, however, and one in the

Jeremiah text that may fit well into a sermon on general suffering (as well as into a sermon on suffering "for the name of Christ"). The promise is made to Rachel that her work will be rewarded. Her work seems to include all that she did in bearing, raising, sorrowing, and interceding for her children and for their descendants. Whatever the relation between her work and her reward, Rachel is told that her yearnings will one day be fulfilled. Intercession can keep hope alive when it is founded on the God who hears and answers. Especially in the times of our anguish we are to trust the words of the Lord: "There is hope for your future."

First Pet. 4:19 insists that suffering is no excuse for not doing "right." The temptation to turn inward, to hide, to take it all out on someone else is to be resisted. The command to love one's neighbor and to do good is always applicable.

The Name of Jesus

JANUARY 1

Lutheran	Roman Catholic*	Episcopal
Num. 6:22–27	Num. 6:22–27	Exod. 34:1–8
Rom. 1:1–7 or Phil. 2:9–13	Gal. 4:4–7	Rom. 1:1–7 or Phil. 2:9–13
Luke 2:21	Luke 2:16–21	Luke 2:15–21

The general observance of this day goes back to the sixth century. It was originally commemorated as the octave (eighth day) of Christmas and was specially dedicated to the Virgin Mary. It was the most ancient of the Marian feasts in the West. In the ninth century the focus of the celebration changed to that of the circumcision and the name of Jesus. These were jointly commemorated until the sixteenth century.

January 1 seems to have been chosen as a feast day in order to combat the unruly celebrations of New Year's Day (in Africa, Italy,

*Octave of Christmas, Solemnity of Mary Mother of God.

Spain, France). Then, as now, the day was marked by general pagan gaiety. At first the councils of the church forbade participation in such festivities. Later the day was set aside as a time of fasting, litanies, and penance, and church attendance became an obligation.

The texts for this day are related by their common reference to "name" and "naming."

EXEGESIS

First Lesson: Num. 6:22–27. The exact origin of this Aaronic benediction is almost impossible to determine. Its language argues for a postexilic date (P narrative), but its simplicity points perhaps to a much earlier beginning. According to Deuteronomic law it was part of the priest's duty to give a blessing to the people (Deut. 21:5). Its place was in the sanctuary, and it was given both as an opening act and as a closing one.

While pronouncing blessing was a function of the priest, it is clear that he was only a mediator. The subject of each clause in vv. 24–26 is "the Lord." It was God who told Moses what Aaron and his sons should say, and it was God who was operative in the saying. The fact that it was God acting in the blessing is further attested by the connection between the blessing and the putting of God's name upon the people (v. 27). The name of God is the being of God himself (everything he has shown himself to be). His name not only distinguishes him, but it also relates people to him by giving them access. When God's name is "laid on the people," an actual power is set in motion. Where his name is, God himself is present in blessing (1 Kings 9:3). To bless with the name of the Lord is to invoke all that God is and has done.

The content of the Aaronic blessing is highly suggestive. Some see in it a germinal form of the Trinity: the Father and preservation (v. 24), the Son and enlightenment (v. 25), the Holy Spirit and peace (v. 26). Others focus on the meanings of its richly textured words and phrases. "Make the face shine" has synonyms in "save," "restore," and "redeem." "Lift up the countenance" (to turn toward someone in friendship) also means "show favor" and is used as an adjective to describe an honored person. "Peace" signifies absolute well-being.

Still others point to the fact that the good gifts of God enumerated in the blessing are gifts for earthly well-being. This at least is the blessing's original sense and the limit of its scope.

Second Lesson: Rom. 1:1–7. This lection was probably selected to be read on this festival because of its reference to "his name" in v. 5. This verse appears in the middle of an expanded letter introduction in which Paul provides a brief yet intricate outline of the gospel. Jesus, descended from David according to the flesh (his lowly, earthly status) and resurrected from the dead by the power of God (exalted status as Son of God), is Lord (the earliest creedal formula). Through the Lord Jesus Christ both Paul and his readers have received grace and have been called to obedience (Paul specifically to the apostolic task of bringing about obedience among the Gentiles, "all nations").

The obedience to which both Paul and his readers have been called is the obedience of faith. It is obedience to the gospel, for the sake of which they have been set apart (v. 1). It is the desire to accept and grasp what is offered in the promise of Christ (v. 2)—the "free gift of righteousness" (5:17). Only such obedience gives due honor to the name of Jesus as Son of God and Son of David, as Lord. Inasmuch as name and being cannot be distinguished, the honor shown by obedience is finally honor to the person of Jesus Christ himself.

Both Paul and his readers "belong" to the Person to whom honor is due. Paul describes himself as a "servant" *(doulos,* "a slave") of Jesus Christ. The primary significance of this word for Paul is that he and all Christians belong (as do also his readers) to their Master. The servant and master live with each other in the closest confidence. The servant is entrusted with the most delicate and confidential mission. The servant lives under the name of his master and carries that name with him wherever he goes.

Second Lesson: Phil. 2:9–13. There is little doubt that this alternative Second Lesson was chosen because of its emphasis on the "name of Jesus." Vv. 9–11 are part of a primitive Christian hymn which begins in Paul's text at v. 6. The hymn is quoted in the middle of an appeal for humility ("Do nothing from selfishness or conceit"— v. 3).

The name bestowed on Jesus is the name "Lord" (v. 11). It is the title of the covenant God of Israel now applied to Jesus (a rendering of the Hebrew *Yahweh* in the Septuagint). It was bestowed on him at his exaltation (resurrection), an exaltation which followed his subordination and obedience (humility) as a kind of inevitable consequence. It is the name which is to be confessed. It includes all that he is and all that he has done. It locates the "glory of God the Father" in the fact that he prepares his kingdom in incomprehensible condescension (Barth).

The RSV translation of v. 5, "which is yours in Christ Jesus" (rather than "which was also in Christ Jesus," ASV), permits an emphasis on Christ as the source of Christian life rather than as an example of it. The "mind of Christ" is a gift rather than a model. The call to humility is more of an indicative than an imperative. Everything signified by the exalted name of Jesus ("Lord") belongs to the Christian who confesses it. The call to humility is a call to the Christian community to live out their lives in conformity with who they are in the humbled/exalted One.

To "work out your salvation" means to work, move, and live as one claimed by the promise of wholeness. In the context of this lection it has a definite social thrust. It means to live in humility (a matter of "fear and trembling") before one another. And it means to have confidence in God while living out such humility. The God who exalted the humble One will support and give help (v. 13).

Gospel: Luke 2:21. This single verse has often been attached to what precedes it (vv. 15–20) and might also be used with the purification event which follows. It seems rather lonely and drab the way it is. The verse carries none of the strong emphasis on naming that its parallel passage does (1:57–64). Even the activity of Jesus' parents is nonexistent. It stands as a simple statement of fact.

The liturgical separation of the naming of Jesus from his circumcision seems to coincide with Luke's emphasis. The stress here is clearly on the naming. This stress highlights the obedience of Jesus' parents to God's word rather than their obedience to the law (Lev. 12:3–4). The name is given in accord with the angel's command at the annunciation.

The name "Jesus" is the Greek equivalent of the Hebrew "Joshua," which was supposed to mean "Yahweh is salvation" (cf. Matt. 1:21). The name thus identifies Jesus as the one in whom the name of God is made clear and present. It announces and sums up the purpose of his birth and of his work.

The definitive Palestinian setting of v. 21 and what follows emphasizes the fact that God's salvation is an act and not a myth. It occurs in human history, in Jesus who was conceived, born, and later circumcised and purified. It is said that Luke had no theology of incarnation, and yet Jesus' solidarity with the human situation is clear.

While the circumcision of Jesus is not the central focus of the text, it is nonetheless included. It has been suggested that theological reflection on circumcision has been both positive and negative. Positively it can be seen as the external sign of membership in the covenant community (Gen. 17:13, the "everlasting covenant" in flesh). Negatively, the rite of circumcision is viewed as superfluous, as having been replaced by the circumcision of faith (Rom. 4:11).

HOMILETICAL INTERPRETATION

Two general foci suggest themselves as appropriate to this day and to its texts. One is the significance of Jesus' name. The other is liturgical activity related to the name of Jesus and to its celebration on January 1. Several possibilities occur for each of these foci.

Scholars warn us that an understanding of the relation between a name and the nature of that which is named can only be gained from a knowledge of primitive belief. That has always seemed to be an overstatement. Or at least the primitive belief spoken of seems much closer than it is sometimes thought to be. It can be experienced, for example, in the literature of the American Indian (N. Scott Momaday is a prime representative). It can also be approached by reflection on our own (nonprimitive) use of names.

Names relate us. How frustrating it is to hang up the phone on an unidentified voice. How beautiful it is when the name of one admired from a distance is suddenly revealed ("I just met a girl named Maria!"). How complete it seems when "baby boy Smith" finally becomes "John."

Names identify us as individuals. W. H. Auden says that proper
names are poetry in the raw—untranslatable. The meanings of words
rarely change over a century, but the meaning of a name can change
because of our contact with one who bears it (there are some names
we just don't like). Memories surround a name because it is in the
name that one is imagined.

Observations such as these may not make primitive belief fully
accessible, but they can help us in grasping some of the claims made
by the texts for this day. God's name relates him to us and us to him.
By his name God is identified. Only God fulfills his name. Only God's
name never changes its meaning. And God's name is Jesus—Lord.
By him we are related to God. By him God is identified. By him God's
unchanging nature is made known—"Yahweh will save," "Yahweh
is salvation."

To confess Jesus Christ as Lord means in part to recognize that he
is the source of our wholeness, that he has done for us what we could
not do for ourselves. The Lord's favor toward us does not depend
upon our loyalty or upon our selflessness or upon our achievements.
Rather his obedience and his humility and his exaltation are ours.
As Jesus' name was given rather than chosen (Luke), just so is the
Lord's name given to us. All he is and all he has done is ours. To
confess Jesus Christ as Lord also means to acknowledge that we
belong to him as a servant *(doulos)* belongs to a master. We are taken
into the closest confidence and entrusted with a mission. We are to
honor his name by obedience.

On the one hand, this obedience to which we are called is the
obedience of faith (Romans). To obey is to have confidence that the
name Jesus, Savior, signifies the true nature and work of its hearer. It
is to accept and grasp the free gift of forgiveness offered by the One
confessed as Lord. It is to look to the name and person of God for all
consolation and to call upon it—him—by invocation and prayer
(Luther). It is to be obedient to God's word by believing it (Luke). On
the other hand, the obedience of believers is the living out of the gift
given (Philippians). To obey is to live with fear and trembling in the
presence of neighbors who need our care. It is to relate to others in
humility, counting others better than ourselves, looking to the interests of others, behaving like a neighbor in active service. It is to

understand Bonhoeffer's propositions: only he who believes is obedient, and only he who is obedient believes.

This festival may be a good occasion on which to talk about the Aaronic benediction. This OT benediction is widely used in unchanged form by the Christian church, and has been for centuries. In some usages it is "Christianized" by the addition of the simple trinitarian blessing "In the name of the Father and of the Son and of the Holy Ghost." In other usages it stands without addition. In both cases, however, the benediction has reached its fullest explication by use in Christian worship. The name of God put on the people by means of the benediction now includes everything that God has done in Jesus. The germinal form of the Trinity found in it has reached its full development. It is now pronounced in light of the full disclosure of God in Jesus (enlightenment) and in light of the gift of the Holy Spirit who gives peace.

The second essential point about the benediction is its function. It is certainly far more than a pious way to close the service. And it is far more than the mutual well-wishes of friends. It is an invoking of the name of the Lord which effects salvation; for where his name is, there God himself is present in blessing. Power is set in motion. (It is the "priest's" duty to give the blessing, but it is God who is operative in it.)

This festival may also be a good occasion on which to talk about baptism. This seems particularly appropriate in a tradition in which baptisms would normally or occasionally occur on the First Sunday after the Epiphany.

Although none of the texts for the day refer to baptism, the baptismal bias of Paul encourages its inclusion (see Rom. 6:3ff.). So do all the references in the texts to "his name." Baptism is effective because God's name is in it—and where God's name is, there must also be life and salvation (Luther). We are baptized in the name of Christ and we are baptized into his name (his person). The Aaronic benediction invokes the name of the Lord upon those who are already within the name. Those who are thus blessed already belong to him.

Our texts also enable us to point on this day to the fact that it is in baptism that we are given our names in Christ. On this day when we recall the giving of his name, we also remember the gift of our own. As his name announces and sums up his identity and meaning, so do our names in Christ announce and sum up our identity and meaning in him.

Perhaps on this festival occasion the secular celebration of New Year's Day (and Eve) should be recognized in a positive way (in spite of the fact that the Christian festival began as a rejection of unruly secular activities). A large part of the New Year's festivities are in celebration of the future's potential. The new year is depicted as a baby—healthy, responsive, unhampered by old doubts and dull routines. The habit of resolutions celebrates the fact that one can begin again, beyond the mistakes and failures of the past. Confetti made from discarded newspapers and calendars announces the rupture of the past's domination.

The church on New Year's Day celebrates the event of which the secular festival is only a dim reflection. The church celebrates the fact that God in Jesus Christ has established the newness of all things and that he has made us new in every relationship. Our baptism in and into the name of Christ constitutes a new birth, a new beginning, a participation in the new age which has appeared within the old. We face a new year as continually new people, both confident and determined that in every act and relationship the gift of newness will be manifest.

The Confession of St. Peter

JANUARY 18

Lutheran	Roman Catholic*	Episcopal
Acts 4:8–13		Acts 4:8–13
1 Cor. 10:1–5	1 Pet. 5:1–4	1 Pet. 5:1–4
Matt. 16:13–19	Matt. 16:13–19	Matt. 16:13–19

The date and title of this festival originate with the Episcopal calendar. Paul has a separate festival on January 25, and the martyrdoms of both Peter and Paul are commemorated on June 29. These two great apostles have been associated in Christian thought and

*Chair of Peter, Apostle, February 22.

worship from earliest times. Their apostleships embraced the church's complete ministry to both the Jewish and gentile worlds. It is fitting that with these two apostles the Week of Prayer for Christian Unity begins and ends: the Confession of St. Peter on January 18, and the Conversion of St. Paul on January 25.

The Week of Prayer for Christian Unity began at Graymoor, Garrison, New York, in 1908. It continues to be what some have called a "permanent dialogue of spirituality which expresses what should happen during the whole year" between Christian communions and communities.

EXEGESIS

First Lesson: Acts 4:8–13. This lection provides a glimpse of the confessing apostle in action. All but v. 8a and v. 13 comprise Peter's first defense-sermon before the high council (the second is recorded in 5:29–32). He and John seemingly had two things to answer for: their preaching of the resurrection (of great offense to the Sadducees— 4:2–3), and the means by which Peter had healed a crippled man (3:1–10). Of prime interest to Peter was the resurrection, which he again proclaimed forcefully after a glancing reference to the healing of the cripple. The rulers and elders were amazed at the apostles' boldness and sureness, particularly because they were unlearned, common men (and because they should have been under severe pressure before such an august body?). Luke tells us that the source of Peter's "boldness" was the Holy Spirit (given as promised in Luke 12: 11–12).

So we see the apostle: healer, preacher of the resurrection, defender of the faith, ordinary but confident, filled with the Holy Spirit. It is difficult to know whether or not the event happened the way Luke wrote it. It has been suggested that he combined an act-of-Peter story with resurrection preaching (which includes familiar Lucan rhetoric—cf. 2:23–24; 3:13ff.). Such an origin would in no way cloud what we see of Peter in what is written.

Luke's central concern in this passage, as elsewhere, is to convince his readers of the apostle's right and duty to preach Christ in spite of all opposition and harassment. It is also his purpose to call his readers to the same task of bearing witness, certain that the promised Spirit will be as present for them in trial as he was for Peter. Of key significance in the preaching is Christ's resurrection. In Peter's speech the rejection/exaltation theme is clearly struck. Rejection and the cross were not the end—even though the Sadducees claimed they were. Jesus has been raised—of this the healed cripple is proof. Jesus is now the keystone without which everything crumbles (Ps. 118:22). In the rejected/exalted "Jesus Christ of Nazareth" alone is there salvation (Christianity is absolute).

Of some interest is the fact that Ps. 118:22 (quoted also in Mark 12:10) is one of the first pieces of Christian apologetic. Of some interest also is the double sense of "name" in the passage. In v. 10 it is used as it might have been in exorcism. In v. 12 it is applied to healing as salvation. Between the two is the account of Jesus' death and resurrection. Healing of the body occurred both before and after the resurrection. Healing as salvation occurs only after the exaltation.

Second Lesson: 1 Cor. 10:1–5. This passage appears elsewhere in the church year as part of a longer reading, namely vv. 1–13 (the Third Sunday in Lent, cycle C). In its abbreviated form it calls attention to overconfidence and to Christ "the Rock." Both foci have application to Peter. The apostle's overconfidence is well documented, particularly in his insistence to Jesus that "even if I must die with you, I will not deny you" (Matt. 26:33–35, followed by the denial in vv. 69–75). There is also the verbal similarity between Christ as Rock and Peter as rock, and the implication of Peter's dependence on Christ (Cephas, by which name Peter is also called in John 1:42 and 1 Cor. 15:5, is the Aramaic equivalent of the Greek *petros* or *petra* which means "rock").

The overconfidence that Paul warns about is connected to the church's position as the true Israel ("our fathers," v. 1, includes both Jewish and gentile readers) and to its sacramental life (baptism and the Lord's Supper, vv. 3–4). He warns that neither election nor sacraments constitute a permanent security against temptation (10:13) or idolatry (10:14). The exodus pilgrims provide Paul with a case study. He claims that the chosen exodus community also had the sacraments (though in an antecedent form) but that they were nonetheless "overthrown in the wilderness" (Num. 14:29–30). Their special status gave them no immunity. Paul's warning against over-confidence gains strength by his inclusion of himself in 9:27 (even he could be "disqualified"). The peculiar temptations and idolatries that confronted the Corinthian community are well documented in chaps. 8—10 (essentially, the lifting up of knowledge and self-regard over love).

In his presentation of the exodus story Paul probably made use of an existing typology, a teaching that predated the writing of the epistle. His interpretation suggests several significant ideas related to the sacraments. The sacraments of baptism and the Lord's Supper are referred to in a single breath; neither one is isolated from, or raised above, the other. The sacraments are designed for nourishment in travel; they are not a goal in and of themselves. While the food and drink in v. 4 are "supernatural" or "spiritual" (that which comes from God and reveals him), they are still food and drink (the reverse is also true).

It is said that the presupposition of Paul's exegesis is the preexistence of Christ. If that is true, the words "the Rock was Christ" have more than symbolic significance. It is further suggested that the "following Rock" (v. 4) is based on an ancient rabbinical tradition which perhaps grew out of the fact that the wilderness rock is mentioned twice in the Pentateuch (Exod. 17:5–6 and Num. 20:1–9).

Gospel: Matt. 16:13–19. The choice of this passage (particularly vv. 17–19) for a festival marking the first day of the Week of Prayer for Christian Unity seems in some respects to be a strange selection. To say that its interpretation has been hotly debated is almost an understatement. Controversy may well have existed in regard to this passage from the beginning. Eduard Schweizer, for example, suggests that vv. 17–19 (early material going back to the Aramaic-speaking church) may represent the Syrian church's declaration of independence from the Jerusalem mother church or (more likely) from the synagogue. Others see the origin of these verses in a heated controversy in the first century between the universalism of Paul and the Jewish restrictions of Peter and others. Today, disagreement continues at key points: Were the keys of the kingdom given to Peter, or to the whole church (or to some combination)? Did Jesus claim that he would build his church on Peter, or on Peter's faith? If Peter was given a specific role in the church that was to be built, what was that role? Did the words to Peter also have Peter's successors in view?

Perhaps the implication of the choice of lection is that controversy should be avoided on this day (if we plan controversy, we shouldn't celebrate the festival). It may point us to those areas of agreement that can be emphasized without compromise (although this may differ with each person). It is clear, for example, that Peter was held in high respect (not only by the community out of which vv. 17–19 originally came, but also by Matthew and his community). It is also fairly clear that the rock was not just the faith of Peter but the person of Peter himself (testified to by his unique position in the primitive Jerusalem church). It is further clear that one aspect of Peter's role was that of witness to the resurrection (noted here in Peter's confession, "You are the Christ, the Son of the living God"—a post-Easter affirmation).

Matthew's revision of Mark 8:27–33 by inserting vv. 17–19 is obvious by simple comparison. Certain other features of the Matthean account are important. Peter's confession marks a turning point (as in the other Gospels). Jesus' attention is now turned toward the preparation of his disciples for the passion. Peter's confession is a gift, a revelation from the Father and not Peter's personal conclusion. The "keys of the kingdom" include teaching authority and disciplinary power. The expression about loosing or binding in heaven further suggests the forgiveness of sins. Death with all its powers (the "gates of Hades" in some translations) will never put an end to the Christian community. The community will survive until the final coming.

HOMILETICAL INTERPRETATION

Sermon possibilities for this day and these texts are numerous. The direction chosen should depend on the congregational context. If the sermon is to be preached at an ecumenical "unity" service, the particular theme should be carefully related to the gathering, its purpose, and the future of dialogue it represents. This theme should be related to the theme planned for the celebration of the Conversion of St. Paul which concludes the Week of Prayer for Christian Unity. If the sermon is to be preached in a single congregation with only its own members present, the theme may well be other than that of unity. A decision might also be based on the number of other Petrine texts that are assigned in the lectionary and on what use is to be made of them during the rest of the year (the Transfiguration of Our Lord, cycles A, B, C; Maundy Thursday, cycle A; the Third Sunday of Easter, cycle C; the Fourteenth Sunday after Pentecost, cycle B; and so forth). It might also make a difference whether or not there have been any baptisms in the congregation during the Epiphany season.

Although the Second Lesson's emphasis on overconfidence may seem like an open invitation to talk about Peter's impetuosity, such a topic should probably be avoided on this day. The lesson from Acts and the Gospel from Matthew cast a light on Peter that shows his strength more than his weakness. And it is good for us to see him in that light. In the text from Matthew we see him as the first disciple to experience the miracle of faith (just as he is listed first among those to whom the resurrected Christ appeared—1 Cor. 15:5). We feel the respect in which he was held by the ancient church. We remember beyond a doubt that his leadership in that church was real and unique (without having to decide on the exact nature of his historical/ecclesiastical role). In the text from Acts we view Peter the unlearned but bold preacher of the cross and resurrection. We see him as healer, defender of the faith, "opportunist" for the gospel. The Apostle Peter has always been one of the most consoling followers of Christ about whom we can talk. He is so human, so much like us in his frailties that we feel there is a chance for our own faithful discipleship. At times perhaps we stress his weaknesses too much. Peter is also a figure of tremendous strength, and he is for our veneration and imitation as well as for our consolation. Whether or not the day is celebrated in an ecumenical context, the place and strength of Peter are worth talking about (even if only as a corrective).

The place to address overconfidence is in regard to ourselves and not in regard to the apostle. This might be particularly true for an ecumenical setting. Even with hearts and minds opened wide by the appeal to unity made by this day and week, we still maintain a good measure of self-regard and "puffed up" knowledge. Deep down we know who has the right church order and the right interpretation of Scripture. Deep down we know whose theological tradition is in line with the Bible and whose history is most undistorted by error. We know whose liturgy is the truest expression of worship "in all times and in all places" and whose musical heritage is the richest and broadest. We know whose pastors are better educated and whose children receive the sturdiest foundation for nurture and growth. *We know. . . !* St. Paul warns us that such "knowledge" gets in the way of love, which means something as concrete as not being an offense to someone else, particularly perhaps by means of our knowledge. He also warns us that such an obstruction of love is not a minor infraction. It is very likely a form of idolatry. Even those things, especially those things which are part of our lives as people of God and nourish us so richly, can become our idols. We can use them to secure our status, to set ourselves apart. We can make them ends in themselves. We can depend on them for our identity. And then they not only get in the way of love, they get in the way of our relationship with God. The things of God in the way of God! Idolatry, Luther says, does not merely consist of erecting an image and praying to it; it is primarily in the heart, the heart which pursues things and seeks help and consolation from sources other than God. Our ecclesiastical, liturgical, theological, administrative knowledge is good, but if it is ever exalted above love it stands to be overthrown.

The church lives under the promise that death will never claim it, that it will survive until the return of Christ. This promise does not mean that the church will never change. It does not mean that the church follows an inevitable line of progress, or that it will never succumb to the temptation of self-reliance and idolatry. It does not mean that any particular congregation or denomination is incapable of dissolution (or even that such a dissolution would necessarily be tragic). In the passage from 1 Corinthians Paul speaks of the church only as a collective unit (he speaks as a Jew to Gentiles and calls them "brethren"; he speaks of the exodus people as the "fathers" of both Jew and Gentile). It is this church that will endure—as it already has for twenty centuries. The church will live forever because Christ lives forever (the centrality of the resurrection in both 1 Corinthians and

Acts). His exaltation signifies the reversal of his rejection. It also
signifies that he lives and works forever (this is the point made by
Peter about the crippled man's healing: "Jesus Christ of Nazareth,
. . . whom God raised from the dead, by him this man is standing
before you well"). As congregations gather to celebrate and pray for
unity, it seems particularly appropriate to remind them of the promise
under which they live, a promise backed by the continuing presence
of the never-dying Christ ("I will build *my* church, and the powers of
death shall not prevail against it"). In part, this means that the church
is free to spend itself, to lose itself, in mission—its preservation never
has been and never will be something under its own control. It may
also be the occasion to say something about the limits of that promise.

The Confession of St. Peter may fall shortly after, or in the middle
of, congregational baptisms or a period of baptismal instruction. If so,
the sermon for the day might well focus on the sacraments. The
Pauline text (1 Cor. 10:1–5) can be particularly helpful even though
Paul's main concern is overconfidence. It seems clear, for example,
that baptism and the Lord's Supper belong together. At least Paul
speaks of them in a single breath (a single sentence). Neither one is
isolated from the other, nor are they prioritized in any way. It also
seems clear that the sacraments were designed for a pilgrim people.
Baptism "into Moses" signified deliverance from bondage (freedom),
and the "supernatural" food and drink meant nourishment along the
way to the land of promise. Just so, Christian baptism effects freedom, and the Lord's Supper sustains the baptized in their travels. In
the broadest sense, the Christian road is the one which extends from
Pentecost to the Parousia. In a more narrow sense, the Christian road
is the road of daily life in which one bears witness to the resurrected
Christ (Acts). The sacraments are designed for the Christian task of
proclaiming the lordship of Jesus, building up the community of
believers, and hastening the coming of God's kingdom of justice,
love, and peace. It also seems quite clear that the sacraments are
never an end in themselves, in the sense that they are to be renewed.
Baptism is not to be repeated, but it is to be renewed daily. A
Christian life is nothing else, Luther says, than a daily baptism, once
begun and ever continued. The Lord's Supper is meant for the fre-
quent nourishment of God's people.

The Conversion of St. Paul

JANUARY 25

Lutheran	Roman Catholic	Episcopal
Acts 9:1–22		Acts 26:9–21
Gal. 1:11–24	Acts 22:3–16 or Acts 9:1–22	Gal. 1:11–24
Luke 21:10–19	Mark 16:15–18	Matt. 10:16–22

The celebration of this festival now concludes the observance of the Week of Prayer for Christian Unity. The facts of its exact origin and development are relatively obscure. The church somehow determined that Paul and Peter should be honored on occasions special to each of them, as well as on the day dedicated to both of them (June 29). The first appearance of the Conversion of St. Paul in the calendar seems to have been in Gaul in the sixth century (some say the eighth century). It later made its way to Rome at some undetermined date (some say the tenth century). The Western church in medieval times apparently found its observance particularly appealing.

Certainly the event commemorated on this day was one of the most significant in the history of the apostolic church. It is related no less than three times in the Acts of the Apostles: 9:1–22; 22:3–16; 26:9–20.

EXEGESIS

First Lesson: Acts 9:1–22. The story told here of Paul's conversion is repeated and supplemented in two later addresses by Paul: as part of his defense "on the steps" in 22:3–16, and as part of his defense before King Agrippa in 26:9–20. The obvious differences and similarities are interesting, and attempts to piece the three reports together provide an occasion for some exciting guesswork. Main attention, however, probably should be on the simple fact that there are three reports and that what they record must be of singular significance. Thus far in Acts the movement of Christianity has been in the direction of the Jews (it has leaned toward them). But now, with the conversion of Saul, the distinctive preparation for the gentile mission begins (v. 15 states the purpose of the conversion clearly). Luke wants to emphasize the fact that the gentile mission was initiated by Christ himself. All three texts demonstrate that neither the conversion nor the mission originated with Saul. Quite the contrary. He was "chosen" as an "instrument" (vessel) to carry out the plan of Christ. Saul's enmity "against the disciples of the Lord" makes Jesus' initiative all the more apparent. Christ guided the gentile mission from the very outset.

Saul's conversion is aptly demonstrated by the narrative. In theological terms, he is crushed by judgment and restored by grace (he dies and is resurrected). The powerful persecutor (breathing threats and clutching mandates that can carry the threats out) is struck helpless by the "light from heaven" ("brighter than the sun"—26:13). Following Jesus' instructions he is led to Damascus where he spends the next three days in fasting (v. 9) and prayer (v. 11), both signs of change. He regains his sight at the hands of the Lord's messenger Ananias, whose understandable hesitancy (vv. 13–14) signifies the tremendous reversal that is to occur. Saul receives the Holy Spirit, is baptized, and immediately begins an unceasing proclamation of the very One he persecuted. In this brief narrative both the mortifying and quickening parts of conversion are apparent. Also apparent is the drastic change of direction and of commitment that conversion entails.

Second Lesson: Gal. 1:11–24. In this lection Paul writes about his conversion and about the events which preceded and followed it. His intention is to answer charges made against his apostleship and the gospel he preached by Judaizers who were "troubling" the Galatians and were seeking "to pervert the gospel of Christ" (v. 7). Since Paul must have received the gospel from the Jerusalem apostles, the Judaizers claimed, he has falsified their teaching by eliminating circumcision as a condition for participation in salvation. In their view, faith in Christ as the Messiah was to be added to salvation by observance of the law. Paul's response is aimed at reestablishing himself as an apostle and reestablishing the gospel of justification by faith (2:16) in the confidence of the Galatians.

Paul insists on his independence from the Jerusalem apostles.

Neither before nor after his conversion was he under their instruction (even his visit to Cephas after three years was more in the nature of a personal visit). Indeed, he had no contact with them at all. His gospel and his commission to preach it came directly from Christ. He was "set apart" for this gospel even before his birth. He needed neither pedagogy nor approval from Jerusalem. His early preaching in Syria and Cilicia was in a region outside the jurisdiction of the apostles at Jerusalem. Even those in Judea who did not know him by sight recognized his authenticity (probably because the opposition to a gospel apart from law had not yet developed).

It is not altogether clear why Paul went into Arabia. The early fathers supposed that the purpose of the travel was to preach. More likely is the suggestion that Paul needed time in isolation with God. (In either case, Paul was not with "men" who could instruct him or supervise his progress.) The gospel Paul received was far more than a mere attachment to, or displacement of, his "former life in Judaism." It was a "revelation" which required an entire restructuring of that which had been before (how firmly he was embedded in his "former life" is demonstrated graphically in vv. 13–14). Paul's time in Arabia may well have been spent in communion with God determining how much of the former life was to be retained, abandoned, or revised.

The exact relation between the events recorded in Galatians and in Acts is difficult to determine. Acts 9 claims that Paul stayed in Damascus following his conversion until he was forced to flee. His first visit to Jerusalem seems to have followed immediately. There is no mention of a three-year stay in Arabia, and the quality of the first Jerusalem visit (Acts 9:26–30) is quite different from Paul's accounting of it in Galatians (1:18–20).

Gospel: Luke 21:10–19. For its use on the Twenty-sixth Sunday after Pentecost, cycle C, this lection is expanded to include vv. 5–9. This extension is helpful because it enables the reader to see vv. 10–11 in their major context, namely, a warning about deceptive signs of the End ("apocalypse now" rather than later seems to be a primary concern of Luke). The central connection between the 10–19 lection and Paul appears in vv. 12–19, focusing as they do on persecution (and Paul, we are reminded, was both persecutor and persecuted). The attachment of vv. 10–11 to vv. 12–19 suggests perhaps that the persecution be seen as a sign of the end time which is both present and future and which signifies that "redemption is drawing near" (21:28).

Vv. 12–19 follow the same basic structure as Mark 13:9–13, but with two interesting omissions. Luke includes no mention of the gentile mission (Mark 13:10), and he omits reference to the Holy Spirit (Mark 13:11). The first omission may be explained by the suggestion that Luke was thinking in vv. 10–11 primarily of the destruction of Jerusalem in A.D. 66–70 (even though his description of persecution points to the church's experience in Acts). The second omission may represent Luke's interest in heightening the christological reference (it is "I," Jesus, who will give you "a mouth and wisdom").

Two types of persecution are described in the passage. The first is that of arrest and trial (v. 12). The second is that of hatred and betrayal, ending for some in death (the reference to "some" softens Mark's account in 13:12). The Christian community is encouraged to see the first type as an opportunity for "bearing testimony." They are not to fear the arrest or trial, not even to the extent of memorizing their defense beforehand. The Lord himself will bear testimony through them with power (v. 15). In regard to the second type of persecution, the Christian community is urged to "endure," to remain unswerved from purpose and loyalty. Some may die, but they will surely participate in eternal life.

It has been suggested that the list of historical disasters enumerated here reflects the events of A.D. 66–70. V. 10 seems to be based on Isa. 19:2 and on 2 Chron. 15:6. V. 11 is typical of apocalyptic (Rev. 6 may be based on the sayings here). It has also been suggested that vv. 12–19 quite probably have a base in the sayings of Jesus (persecution was present from the very beginning). These sayings have been elaborated in the passage in the light of events that actually occurred within the early Christian community.

HOMILETICAL INTERPRETATION

The choice of a theme for this day will probably depend on the particulars of the celebration. An ecumenical setting on an occasion which concludes the Week of Prayer for Christian Unity will suggest certain possibilities. An observance limited to a single congregation will suggest others. In either case, the festival should not pass without some honor paid to Paul. The veneration of Paul (and the Christ he preached) and aspects of the Christian life are both potential subjects.

In his work as an apostle, Paul lived out both types of persecution described by the evangelist Luke (Luke 21:12–19; also "predicted" in Acts 9:16). The addresses by Paul which repeat and supplement the narrative of his conversion (Acts 22:3–16; 26:9–20) were both given during the time of his persecution (arrest and trial). Furthermore, while Paul was not "delivered up" by the troublesome Judaizers in Galatia, he was certainly under accusation from them and felt it necessary to defend himself as if he were on trial. Again, it is almost certain that Paul suffered the persecution of death in Rome at the time of Nero. Without stretching the facts, we can also say that the arrest and imprisonment related in Acts followed accusations made by Paul's "brothers and friends" ("Jewish pilgrims"). In both persecutions Paul withstood the temptations Luke warned against. He did not shrink from bearing witness, and he remained unswerved from his purpose and loyalty.

To call Americans to follow Paul's example as persecuted believers doesn't seem to make much sense. One can urge steadfastness in proclaiming Christ, but without the backdrop of forceful opposition even such proclamation seems tame. Of course, if one were to proclaim Christ's kingdom as a kingdom of justice, love, and peace—and live out the life of that kingdom in all the complex relationship of American society—persecution of some sort might well follow. And of course, if one were to bear an intense witness to the church that it can—should—must—give up its life in service to the world instead of constantly investing, hoarding, and reserving what it has for itself, some sort of "betrayal" might also well occur. The early persecutions came about because the preached gospel (in Paul's case, justification by faith) attacked the precise stronghold of enmity (in Paul's environment, justification by law). Perhaps persecution, itself a sign of the kingdom, would occur if the gospel which is preached today attacked its enemy more precisely and directly. Justice, peace, a life thrown away in compassion, a life of total anticonsumerism—these come close.

Whether or not we personally ever face persecution, the fact is that many Christians today do face hostility, betrayal, arrest, imprisonment, and death because of their witness. And we are united with them in the one church established through the preaching of Paul (so states the collect). The celebration of the conversion of Paul is a good time to remember the various conditions of Christian brethren throughout the world. It is also an appropriate time to remember with thanksgiving that Paul's Christian beginnings were our own. His election as an apostle to the Gentiles had us in mind. We are the Gentiles (Acts 9:15; Gal. 1:16) for whose sake Paul was chosen and for whose salvation he labored so unswervingly.

It is appropriate on this festival also to express gratitude for the gospel which Paul preached. The texts do not allow more than a minimal exploration of that gospel, but its content is implied by the context within which Paul's words in Galatians rest. "A man is not justified by works of the law but through faith in Jesus Christ" (Gal. 2:16). One becomes right with God only by faith in Christ and not by the performance of the external requirements of the law (ritual observance, traditions). There is only one gospel, Paul insists, and this is it. Anything else which goes by the name of gospel is a perversion.

Any celebration of Paul is finally a celebration of Christ. Whether we talk about Paul's steadfastness, or his status as "father of the gentile church," or the gospel that Paul preached, we finally talk about Jesus Christ. Paul was but a "chosen instrument" (Acts 9:15), a tool or implement. Both his selection (before he was born) and his conversion were by the pleasure of God (by "grace"—Gal. 1:15–16). His mission was instituted by the resurrected Lord, and it was the resurrected Lord's presence that gave power to his preaching. When we honor Paul and what we have received through him, we honor Christ and his grace toward us. The oneness of the church may have been established through Paul's preaching, but the church's unity is in Christ himself. Paul may have preached the pure gospel, but Christ is the gospel he preached.

Paul's call was an unprecedented one, and his conversion was as unique as it was dramatic. It would be dangerous to guess the subjective components of Paul's experience on the Damascus road. It would also be dangerous to suggest that Paul's experience is in any way a